City Streets
to
Sussex Lanes

David Johnston

This book is dedicated to my wife Sue,
my brothers, and to the memory of my mother Nellie
and stepfather Harry Pateman

ISBN 978-0-9559006-4-8

Published by Pomegranate Press
Dolphin House, 51 St Nicholas Lane, Lewes, Sussex BN7 2JZ
telephone: 01273 470100; email: sussexbooks@aol.com
website: www.pomegranate-press.co.uk

By the same author (with Annabelle Hughes):
West Sussex Barns & Farm Buildings
Dovecote Press ISBN 1-9043490-0-5

British Library Cataloguing-in-Publication Data.
A catalogue record for this book is available from the British Library.
Printed by Digital Book Print, Milton Keynes MK1 1DR

Preface

by Kim Leslie
West Sussex Record Office

This is one man's journey back into the bitter-sweet memories of a Sussex childhood some fifty years ago. When no home meant sleeping rough on Bognor beach. When no home – out of desperation – meant the cold grey misery of a nearby Victorian workhouse. When no home forced his mother into working as a cook-housekeeper for a rough and ready farmworker. She eventually married him, and so we follow his restless ways from one job to another, from one tied cottage to another, his new family in tow.

David Johnston's story tells of his tough – but happy – childhood with his new stepfather in the Sussex countryside of the 1950s. The old farms and cottages where he lived are affectionately remembered with all their sounds and smells, sometimes even horrors, like the tumble-down hovel of a cottage near Petworth ('the coldest, most inhospitable house I ever entered') where he learnt to cure his warts with the slime of a white slug. We follow his adventures down country lanes, through woodland walks and field paths, revelling in his delight with the wildlife and the country characters he met on the way.

Capturing moments of sheer ecstasy in David's hands can reach lyrical heights. The 'unaccountable stillness' of warm summer days – 'a pause in the soft breathing of the land'; the beauty of birdsong; the hidden mysteries of an old mill-race with its play of light at sunset. This is a sheer love affair with the countryside, with deep affection and curiosity for the quiet, unhurried world around him.

Some of his characters might well have stepped straight out of *Cold Comfort Farm*.* Like doughty Mrs Carver, more a veteran flying ace than a cottager, in bomber jacket, skullcap and goggles from the First World War, charging through the woods, dodging trees at break-neck speed on her ancient motor bike. Nellie, David's mother, had a passion for collecting odds and ends, which filled every nook and cranny of their home – so they lived among old skulls, fossils, stuffed birds and animals, even a pygmy alligator, their glass eyes lit up at night by the dancing flames from the huge log fire. Then there was stepfather – 'Old Harry' or 'Pop' – whose clothes, reeking of the smells of the farmyard, contaminated the whole house, and whose idea of a joke was to shovel spoonfuls of salt into the family's tea cups, dropping his false teeth into his own to make sure nobody took his! His cure for chilblains was a chamber pot full of urine as a foot-bath, always used in the kitchen: 'The rank-smelling slops rained down on the stone-slabbed floor, where they formed tiny pools on the uneven surface.'

Leaving school at fifteen with no academic qualifications, David first worked on a farm, but at seventeen he left for better prospects as an engineering apprentice in Horsham. Here ends his early country memories.

Half a century after leaving his rural roots, David returns to the countryside he loved, noting – with dismay – the vast changes that have transformed his boyhood haunts: the loss of the old working farms, the idyllic country cottages that have been demolished, the fields that now lie barren, the decline of so many species of butterflies, insects and songbirds. Today, with empty barns, cow-yards a tangle of briars, milking parlours eerily quiet, there is 'an

---

* Cold Comfort Farm *by Stella Gibbons, first published in 1932, is a much reprinted classic comedy of rural life set in Sussex. David's stepfather, old Harry Pateman, would have been perfectly at home with the earthy Starkadders.*

uncomfortable emptiness', a quite different sort of silence from the stillness of the warm summer nights of his boyhood, 'a silence so intense' that these sad abandoned buildings 'gave the impression of shouting a soul-destroying scream'.

If there is any one message from all these losses that David writes about so movingly, it is surely that we should care so much more for the land and its farms before it is too late. The causes of agricultural distress lie far beyond David's countryside and far outside his own remit in writing what is a very honest account of what he saw – and what he sees – around him; a personal account of two very distinct journeys in a life so full of rich and rewarding experiences.

For this, and his delightful evocation of the countryside half a century ago, we are all in David's debt. Here is a story certainly worth the telling, but it is much more than just a good story. This is about the reality of living in tied farm cottages in remote parts of rural Sussex in the 1950s, about a way of life now gone for ever. Through David's writings we can enjoy its sunshine, and despair at its storms.

Tony (left) and David

Author's notes and acknowledgements

Some of the places and names of people in this book have been changed.

I would like to thank my son Daniel, daughter-in-law Debbie and cousin Ian Cairns for their technical help and advice with the complexities of my computer.

Many thanks also to Kim Leslie of the West Sussex Record Office for his invaluable advice, and to John Kay of the Ringmer History Study Group for his help in adding extra information to the old 'duelling soldiers' story.

Special thanks must go to my wife Sue, for her support, patience and time spent typing my manuscript for this book.

Contents

1 City Streets 5

2 To Sussex Lanes 15

3 Harry Unearths a Bomb 23

4 Mixing the Christmas Pudding 27

5 Selling Flowers by the Roadside 31

6 The Return to Dial Post 34

7 Clay Hill Farm, Ringmer 36

8 Black Tea in the Cornfields 43

9 A Ghostly Visit 50

10 Threshing the Corn 57

11 The Floods Are Up 60

12 The Return to Ringmer 63

13 Lowfold Farm 65

14 The Dog's a Thief 70

15 A Great Knot of Snakes 73

16 The Return to Lowfold 75

17 The Homely Old Farmhouse 77

18 The Foxhunt Runs Riot 86

19 A Long-Lost Mill 88

20 A Boat Trip Turns Sour 93

21 Woodland Rides on a Motorbike 95

22 A Farm Auction 99
23 Guy Fawkes Night 101
24 The Return to Freehold. 105
25 The Cottage on the Hill 110
26 The Art of Hand-milking 114
27 Gathering Fruit 118
28 The Labouring Giant Picks a Fight. 121
29 The Return to Westlands 124
30 Juppsland Farm, Adversane 126
31 The Gypsy Camp. 130
32 A Fatal Disease in the Cows 135
33 A Return to Country Lanes 137

1 City Streets

When a boy, I came out of the city and was touched by the spell of the land, the beauty of the county I had come to live in. There, fresh from the town, the tarmac roads, I looked on in wonder at the countryside about me. So great was the contrast, the wild lush country compared to those city streets, that I could never have dreamt in those infant years that such a world lay out there.

Now, as I look back, I wonder too at the unforeseeable twists that life takes on its route through time, those distant, often harsh days of childhood, when first we left our urban terraced house. There was no indication as to the path destiny was to take us. As a family, we had been cast in the cold, comfortless sink hole of existence, following the early death of my father.

They said he was a cockney, born within the sound of Bow Bells. Yet, following a long illness with cancer, he had died in a hospital on the south coast leaving my mother penniless. Evicted from her rented town house in Chichester, she hastily stored her furniture, then fled back to London to stay with a sister-in-law in Forest Gate. Here, my brother Tony, then eleven years old, and I, three years younger, attended the local school. We had long since settled into the routine, but it was not to last. Events were about to take place that would alter the course of our lives in such a way that we could never have imagined the eventual outcome.

The day that culminated in this profound change sticks indelibly in my mind, for it was the last time we were to attend that place of early learning. The final lesson was physical training, the topic being every boy's favourite, boxing. We all took turns, a single bout each, until the whole class had tried their fighting skills. My chance soon came round and I leapt into the ring to face my rival, our courage boosted by the cheers of our school chums. The master, acting as referee, set the match going with a resounding clang of the assembly bell. In that instant, an eruption of fists exploded in my face. I staggered back, regained my feet, then returned a similar flurry of blows, much to my opponent's disgust.

"Gar'on, smack 'im in the mouth! Gar'on, give it to 'im proper!" echoed the voices of the whole form, in their East London accents.

The bout was soon over. I skipped down from the platform, my eyes smarting from the pounding they had taken. The assembled school friends broke into two groups, each cheering their respective heroes. Then, as if by an unseen command, they turned their hoots of enthusiasm to the next two contestants. A few brisk rounds later and school closed for the day.

I scampered up the street to my old aunt's home, my brother by my side. There, we walked into a raging row that had blown up between my mother and her sister-in-law. The substance of the uproar was that we could no longer stay at the flat, the place being far too small.

"Besides," the aunt raved, "the landlord has threatened to evict me if you stay any longer!"

David and Tony Johnston, 1949

"But I've got nowhere to go! And what about the kids? What am I to do with them?" my mother yelled.

"I don't know! But you gotta go, Nell, or we'll all be chucked out!"

There was no reasoning between the two women. By the following morning we were out and on the road.

The first few hours of that bitterly cold December day we spent wandering the city streets, lost among the invisible vagabonds of London. Then, with the approach of afternoon, my mother made up her mind to make our way back south. The long trudge through the streets was saved to some extent by the gallant act of a cheerful lorry driver, who, going in the same direction, took us as far as Bognor Regis, where we arrived by nightfall.

We shuffled along the dark, wet promenade, the constant rhythm of the foaming sea beating on the shingle. That was the first time I sensed the intense desperation within my mother. I squeezed her hand reassuringly, looked up at her, then over to my elder brother. No words were spoken: there seemed no point. The harshness of our predicament, our very destitution, was only too apparent, even to the mind of a child. The Christmas lights glowing in the sea-front windows caught my attention. An overwhelming sense of dejection swept through me, a fearful feeling of not belonging to that world with its bright neon lustre. I looked away, my eye's falling on the blaze of reflections that shimmered deep in the channel of the damp, tarmac road.

We slipped down a dozen steps to the gloom of the beach walkway and there found shelter from the icy wind in an arched alcove. Settling down for the night on the stone floor, I snuggled close to the bosom of my mother, a coat shielding my back from the December tempest that whistled through the black gaping entrance.

That night the cold concrete floor rose up and gnawed into the very bones of my body, while the damp air cloaked my exposed frame, saturating it in freezing beads. I shivered uncontrollably, slept fitfully, the incessant scraping of shingle, the pounding of waves on the shore, ever present in my conscious moments.

The harshness of that night cut deep into my mind and my soul. For, in later life, and even now, whenever I see a tramp, a man of the road, I see a fellow sufferer and dig into my pocket to pass him a few coins in memory of all that occurred on that dreadful morning.

We dragged our stiff bodies back to the promenade and were there confronted by a policeman on a bicycle, a kindly man, one of the old school, who expressed a deep concern for my mother and her two young waifs. He pointed out the existence of sheltered accommodation a few miles further up the coast, then put his hand in his pocket and gave her half a crown, to buy hot tea and to help us on our way.

Two hours later and there we stood, looking up at the massive grey building that was the main block of the Victorian workhouse at East Preston. Our rooms were in the one time stable block belonging to that institution, then converted to chalets for homeless families.

Entering through a large pair of shabby green doors, we walked into a cobbled yard where, above, stretched a series of clothes lines, each attached to the eaves of the old loose boxes that enclosed the yard. Sheets and shirts flapped in the chill breeze, each garment stained with blotches of purple, as if with blackberry juice. "Iodine," my mother explained, a remedy dabbed on the sores of the impetigo that plagued the family in the chalet opposite. Closing the door on the bitter wind, we lit the tiny oil stove heater and drank hot tea to warm our insides. The woven hemp carpet that covered the floor, and the bare, green walls were of no matter to us then, as we sipped from our steaming cups.

That night we pulled back the sheets that covered our iron beds with expectations of luxurious sleep. But it was not to be, for the institution's fleas more than welcomed the new arrival of the incoming flesh. The hemp carpet was host to an infestation of the pests that consistently plagued our beds, forcing a nightly ritual of flea killing before we could retire.

As dawn broke that first morning in the workhouse I scratched furiously at the rash of bites that covered my body. My eyes wandered with despair over to my mother, who was busy lighting the tiny stove that stood in the centre of the room.

"I will have to go out," she said gravely, dark frowns on her face displaying the depth of her concern.

"There's no food! I'll have to pawn some clothes," she continued, directing her words to my elder brother. "So look after your brother while I'm gone."

12

"How long ya gonna be Mum?" he groaned.

"Not long, I hope. I should be back later this morning. Behave yourselves while I'm out."

The little oil stove was beginning to radiate the merest glimmer of heat when, with a bundle under her arm, she made her way out into the chill of that morning. The hours ticked by, passing midday, and still we waited, our empty bellies aching. We wandered time and again through the cobbled yard and out through the green doors to the road, repeatedly looking first one way up the street, then the other. The afternoon dragged on and it was fast growing dark when at last we saw with relief the shadowed silhouette of her figure walking towards us, the bundle of clothes she had carried out that morning gone.

Potatoes, carrots, meat, bread and butter were placed on the table. We eyed them hungrily. The preparation of that desperately essential hot meal began, the gas stove in the tiny box-sized kitchen spurring the saucepans to the boil. The table was laid, and we

The East Preston Workhouse, c. 1905, founded 1792, rebuilt 1873, demolished 1969

eagerly pulled up our chairs while our motherly cook flitted in and out of the kitchen to inspect the boiling vegetables. Returning after half a dozen visits, she flew over to her handbag and turfed out the contents onto the bed.

"The gas has gone, and I haven't got any money left for the meter!" she cried.

The potatoes were hurriedly placed on the oil heater in an effort to keep them boiling. We waited and waited, but it was no use: the water went off the boil and the veg remained uncooked. That night we went to bed with no more than a sandwich of bread and butter. There were many such days to come before we were to leave that cold grey building, and Christmas day in that institution was no exception.

With early spring, a slender ray of light shone hope on those dark, bewildering times. My mother had noticed in the vacancies page of the county newspaper an advert for a live- in housekeeper. In reply she had written a short explanation of our situation, to which an invitation came back for an interview, and she was to "bring along your two children".

2 To Sussex Lanes

In spite of the late morning sun the haw frost still spread white across outlying fields and clung to the branches of trees that flanked the narrow country lane we walked with breathless anticipation. We passed Swallows Farm which lay up on a hill, then soon came in sight of our destination, Cherry Tree Cottage, Dial Post.

The old dwelling lay on its own, beside the road, with lush green meadows to the rear and ancient woodland further afield. A pair of cherry trees stood like sentries each side of the wicket gate, with a smooth stone path that curved a picturesque route to the front door.

As we came into the garden we were greeted by a clean shaven countryman of average height, who introduced himself as Harry Pateman. He made clear the position he offered, as we stood there on the path. He was a farm worker, he explained, a cowman who worked on the farm up the lane, so could offer no money, only accommodation in return for a live-in cook-housekeeper.

"I'm separated from me wife!" he said, closely observing her reaction, and then continued, "I'm waitin' for a divorce and me two boys are in a children's 'ome!"

My mother thought over the situation, considered her options, then happily agreed to take the job, but on one condition only, "that my children remain with me." Harry nodded his head in agreement as he ushered her towards the house and through the front door.

"Not much furniture," he said apologetically as we walked into the low beamed front room. "Left all I 'ad with the wife when I walked out on 'er," he continued, "but will soon get some more if'n you moves in."

He threw a couple of logs on the fire with some force, as if to emphasise the strength of his words. The embers instantly drew up, spitting sparks across the bare oak floor, while flames curled up the black mouth of the chimney.

I edged closer to the warmth of the hearth. How homely that old house seemed to me that day, in spite of there being scarcely any furniture in the rooms.

Ice that covered the hedgerows of the garden had barely thawed before darkness fell to another freezing night. Candles were lit, and the room took on an appearance that would have been familiar to farm labourers a couple of hundred years ago. The fire licked strange shadows on the walls and sporadically lit up the faces of my mother and Harry, who sat on a couple of old boxes and talked in low pleasing voices way into the evening.

A calm feeling of security flowed through me when I heard him agree in his deep earthy voice that we could "all stay and sleep the night". And sleep we did. A coat covering my body, I lay on the bare floor beside the warm fire, my mother and brother by my side – a peaceful, hallowed sleep.

The friendly old house I came to know and love in the two years we lived there. During this time our furniture was retrieved from storage; Harry's two young boys, Jim, aged 6 and Billy, a year younger, were brought home to his care; and my mother, by way of convenience, finally married the countryman.

"Old Harry," as we affectionately called him when not in earshot, but "Pop" to his face, proved to be a character of the old country breed. He rose from farm labourer to cowman in his life span, was typically Sussex in a stubborn way, yet lumbered with a fitfully restless nature that prevented his holding a job down for more than a year or two at any time. He rarely shaved more than once a week, and would incessantly puff spasms of smoke from the corner of his mouth, vigorously sucked from an old pipe that seemed a permanent fixture.

His simple humour often fuelled hearty laughter that forced the relic to be snatched from his mouth, while throwing back his head and erupting into uproarious guffaws. This outburst was usually the result of some practical joke with which he had a fondness to play at opportune moments.

His new wife was of a quieter nature, more studious, in fact of remarkable contrast. For my mother was a curious woman, in that her natural passion for the countryside inspired her to collect and press many different species of wild flowers that she gathered while out on walks. Each specimen was then meticulously placed and named in scrap-books which, over the years, amounted to a considerable number of volumes. Not content with this, her ever inquisitive mind induced her to study archaeology, the knowledge gleaned from books bought for a few pennies at junk sales. Her lifetime collection of relics included a number of flint and iron arrow heads, a beautifully polished flint axe head, a quern stone, a genuine Pyecombe shepherd's crook and numerous stuffed birds in glass cases. Her hoard of museum bits sadly diminished over the years due to the necessity of having to sell various pieces when money was short in the house.

Nellie & Harry Pateman, 1954

Making ends meet seemed always to be a struggle, in spite of the seemingly endless amount of time spent in the garden growing our own vegetables. In addition we had free milk from the farm and sufficient wood for the fires in the house.

The cordwood, piled up in the garden to the rear of the red brick shed, always required sawing into logs, a daily chore constantly dished out to Old Harry's stepchildren. He would come in from work and grumble that we had to do our share about the house.

"Come on you boys! Go an' saw some wood up for yer mother," he would moan. As we were youngsters, any protest would have been futile, so we would light the old paraffin lantern and head reluctantly out to the shed.

"Lazy old sod! Why don't he do it 'imself?" Tony would mumble quietly under his breath as we wandered into the dark shadows of the outhouse.

The lamp would be hung on a nail on the beam and, with the great cross-cut saw that Harry had shown us how to use, we would soon build up the log pile. Armfuls would be brought into the kitchen and stacked by the old black range, the hungry burner eating a daily supply throughout the year. A kettle perched half on the hot plate of this old cooker incessantly hissed and fumed, announcing its presence to those who walked through the room

Billy, Mum, Pop and Jimmy

18

during the quiet hours of the day. Its miniature juddering, its constant fidgeting, always gave the impression it was impatient to please parched throats with hot tea.

In a gloomy corner of the room stood an oak table with half a dozen chairs placed round where sat my stepfather, mother and their four sons for each evening meal, always eaten in silence. For Harry's views on table manners were strictly of a Victorian nature, the enforced rule often inducing much suppressed humour among the four boys. The slurping, burping, supping, sipping, scraping of knives and forks, clanking of cups, together with Old Harry's laboured breathing (a result of years of smoking), was deafening in the quietness of the room. It was not unusual for a lively imagination to conjure up some comic scene in such conditions, resulting in a quivering smile forming on tense lips. The appearance of this involuntary smirk would be instantly infectious to all those at the table. An uncontrollable burst of giggling would then erupt, only to be cut short by the old man.

An amusing incident occurred around the first summer we were with old Harry, the principal character in the scene being my uncle Bert. A keen cyclist, he had peddled down from London on a planned visit to our tied cottage, his first meeting with Harry. It was mid-afternoon when he arrived. The strenuous bike ride had by all accounts given him a ravenous appetite and he looked eagerly forward to the evening meal. He took his place at the table opposite the old man, a steaming dish was put in front of him and he soon began shovelling the food into his mouth in a breathless fashion, his eyes glued to the plate. Old Harry, in his slow and deliberate way, looked up and observed with annoyance the speed with which our hungry visitor was disposing of his dinner and said, with a note of sarcasm, "Going by train then?"

"No!" replied Bert, innocently "I've got my bike outside!"

We all burst into spontaneous laughter, except for the old man.

Harry was not always so severe. There were times when his simple humour was more than apparent to those who were the butt of his jokes. We would settle down at the table in readiness for a meal, my mother busily pouring each of us a steaming mug of tea, while the old man eyed her every move, a roguish smile apparent on his face.

With the tea poured, we would take the first sip or two, only to be thrown into alarm by one or the other leaping up and bounding over to the kitchen sink to spit out the mouthful of hot drink. Old Harry, who had secretly shovelled several spoonfuls of salt into the cup, would grip his sides and erupt into uncontrollable laughter at the desired result. During this rousing outburst, his beaming face revealed two rows of finely placed ivory teeth.

These teeth were, in fact, dentures – a false set that he had used since a gum complaint had forced such requirements when a young

Harry Pateman in jovial mood, hoeing the garden.
Note the 'L' plate stuck to his back, and his old pipe – 'a permanent fixture'

man. From that day on he had never bothered to have a replacement set made. They had become old and worn out. Consequently the stem of the pipe that he constantly gripped between these teeth to vigorously suck had, through persistent use, worn a hole in the sharp, biting edge. This gap, so instantly noticeable whenever he laughed, was of such a size that you could easily drop a pea through the cavity without his ever having to open his mouth. It was as if a black hole had been purposely painted on the two rows of teeth, to give the impression of a comical mask, like that of a clown. There was, for those who noticed this dark, gaping entrance, the chance for a moment's innocent amusement, an impulsive snigger that was often difficult to contain during that instant of light-hearted mirth amongst his four sons.

These decrepit dentures, that might have been of scientific interest to any museum, he would often extract and drop mischievously into his steaming mug of tea. This done, he would then rise from the table and trot off to an adjoining room, perhaps on some essential errand.

"That'll make sure none of you's drinks me tea while I'm gone!" he would chuckle.

On returning, he would dip his leathery thumb and forefinger into the hot drink, fish out the tacky plates and swiftly replace them back in his mouth.

"Oh! I do wish you wouldn't be so disgusting!" my mother would say, mortified by his low form of humour.

The first time my mother and her two sons took his afternoon tea to him, carried steaming hot in an old white enamel 'pint' milk can, was when we first discovered the comic devil in him.

My mother led the way up the lane to the farmyard, her eldest son in tow. I wandered on behind, pausing occasionally to scuff my feet through muddy puddles in idle amusement. A few chickens strutted about the yard, their soft cackling erupting into alarm at our approach. They scattered in all directions. We peered into the great oak barn that served as the milking parlour: cows patiently waiting their turn for milking, stood in a row contentedly chewing the cud. Wandering down the line of beasts we searched for the dairyman, my elder brother leading the way, my mother making our arrival known by bawling out, "Coooee! We've brought your tea up for you, Harry!"

My brother carried on in the lead, then suddenly leapt back in alarm as a jet of milk caught him in the face. Old Harry, hidden from view until then, burst into great guffaws of laughter and almost toppled off his milking stool as he continued to squirt milk over the lad from the teat of the cow.

3 Harry Unearths a Bomb

Swallows Farm in those days still employed many of the old ways of farming, and I look back with fond memories at the times spent there in my childhood. But that which gave the most delight was to wander the fields and lanes with my brothers as companions. The newly discovered freedom, so immeasurably contrasting to those confined city streets, was to me much like being released from a concrete cage. To scamper out of the door of a morning and bound off across the meadows, the sweet spring air brushing my face, the summer months free from the bondage of school, was for sure my greatest pleasure.

The time was often occupied by our favourite diversion of bird nesting. On one particular May morning we set off along the paths in pursuit of eggs, our route taking no particular direction. Soon we came to the River Adur, where close by loomed the solitary fragment of Knepp Castle, an ancient hunting lodge of the de Braose family. We dawdled on, skylarking in boyish games as brothers will. A short distance on, a pollarded willow came into view hanging low over the river. Its branches trailed in the water to act as a natural anchor for the coot's nest that was intricately attached. My elder brother shinned half up the tree to get a clearer view.

"It's got eggs in it!" he shouted, but admitted that it would be difficult to get to without falling in the water.

"That's all right, Tone! I'll go, it'll take my weight!" I yelled back, edging gingerly out on the slender branch before he had time to protest. As I reached over to grasp an egg the willowy bough bent almost double, and in I went. Unable to swim, I panicked, went fully under, took a choking mouthful of water, bobbed up, then desperately lunged for a sinewy twig that held me steady in the swirling currents.

"Here, catch my hand," bawled Tone as he reached out to help me climb back on to the river bank. "You alright?" he continued.

"Yeah, I think so," I gasped. "But the waters freezing!"

There I stood cold, miserable, saturated to the skin, my teeth chattering.

"You was lucky to get out!" Jim said, gripping my shoulder with brotherly affection.

"I know. But how can I get dry?" I moaned. "I can't go home like this, with me clothes dripping wet. The old man'll go mad!"

"Take 'em off and throw 'em over the hedge to dry!" chorused my brothers. The scheme seemed the only thing to do, so I went along with the idea and stripped naked, laying the soaking garments over a thickset hawthorn.

For several hours we lay on the riverbank, the warm south-west breeze soon drying my pale naked body. We chatted, laughed, looked up at the deep blue of the sky, and watched the reflections of cotton wool clouds in the water and the mayflies skipping from reed to reed. The clothes dried, almost, and four hungry brothers trudged home, a hot meal and bath awaiting them.

The once-a-week bath night took on the appearance of a major operation. A narrow, galvanised tub was retrieved from where it hung on a nail outside the back door and placed on the floor in the kitchen. All available saucepans, kettles, cauldrons, pots, pans – in fact anything that held liquid – bubbled and steamed on the range, a dense mist forming in the way that it does in an old ship's boiler room. The combined volume of water from these vessels barely filled the flat-bottomed tub above three or four inches. Consequently, there was the rare occurrence of four young boys fighting to be first in the bath: the longer down the line you were, the colder and dirtier the water was when your turn came. As each of us was scrubbed clean, we would await the other, then troop upstairs to bed, the leader holding the old white enamel 'wee Willie Winkie' style candlestick, shielding the flame from the draught as he went.

An old mahogany chest of drawers stood between two iron beds in our room: one double, shared by the three youngest children, and a single where my eldest brother slept. Once in bed we would read by candlelight, whisper among ourselves or play quietly the game called animal silhouettes. The shadow of a crocodile, elephant, antelope or some such beast would creep up and across the bedroom ceiling.

"Hey, guess what this is?" my eldest brother would chuckle, holding a contorted hand in front of the candle that cast strange shadows on the walls and ceiling.

"That's easy, Tone. It's a rabbit," we would whisper, jumping silently out of bed to each take our turn at the game. This would go on until we tired of the amusement or, as often happened, the old man would shout up to us, "Get to sleep, you boys!"

The only other item of furniture in the bedroom was the chamber pot. Beautifully decorated in a floral design, it was always kept under the bed, strictly for the convenience of the waterworks. Those requiring to do anything other had to use the outside toilet situated at the far end of the garden, an undesirable trip in the short, cold days of winter. Brick-built in the style of a sentry box, it housed a sizeable bucket with removable seat to enable the receptacle to be emptied as required. The old man always carried out this unenviable job once a week, emptying the foul smelling container into a deep pit he had prepared in the garden for this purpose.

On one particular occasion, when digging a fresh hole, he unearthed an unexploded incendiary bomb. The live, but rusting shell was around twelve or fourteen inches in length, with four tail fins and a blunt nose. This deadly missile he clasped in his arms and came running indoors to my mother, excited at the idea he had of adding it to her growing collection of antique artefacts.

"Take the damn thing out doors and get rid of it!" she demanded, angry that he had been so foolish as to even think of bringing it into the house.

In his simple way of dealing with things, the old man dropped this highly dangerous bomb into our large water butt at the rear of the house, and there it stayed.

He was, for sure, a strange character with, at times, peculiar ideas. One Sunday morning we came downstairs to find him astride a chair in the kitchen, bathing his feet in urine. He had one foot squeezed inside the chamber pot, the other by all accounts, had "been done" earlier. My mother worked round him, busily preparing the breakfast.

"Morning Pop!" I said as I came into the room. "What ya doing?"

"Bathing me chilblain's boy!" he replied, with a look of self indulgence. "It's the only thing that seems to do 'em any good these cold days!"

We stared in a strangely amused disbelief, as he raised the saturated limb and shook it vigorously. The rank-smelling slops rained down on to the stone-slabbed floor, where they formed tiny pools on the uneven surface.

"Ah! That's better!" he sighed, as he pulled a sock over his wet toes and up past his ankles.

The fascination that the event had drawn then came to an end. We wandered off to the front room.

"Dirty old bugger!" whispered Jim, when out of earshot.

"Turned me off my breakfast," I said under my breath.

"Yeah! And nearly made me retch," joined in Tony. "If I'd 'ave bin sick I'd have done it all over 'is foot! Bet he wouldn't have suffered from chilblains then!"

We all chuckled quietly at the very thought of such a thing.

This strange habit of the old man's was something we eventually got used to, for each winter he would come in from work, slip off his boots and warm his cold, damp feet by the fire. This would set his chilblains off, and in a week or two out would come the pee pot, in would go each foot, and relief from the constant itching would become noticeably apparent. No more would he be seen incessantly scratching the arches of his corn-infested feet.

4 Mixing the Christmas Pudding

With the settling in to our new way of life in the countryside came the inevitable renewal of our education. Situated in the hamlet of Dial Post, the one-roomed Victorian school we plodded the half mile to each morning was the very picture of a tiny chapel. The single classroom was divided by an enormous maroon velvet curtain, with eight or ten children in the upper section and half a dozen in the lower.

The rather severe looking master took the older infants' lessons. His seemingly strict disciplinarian style of teaching I soon discovered in the first few weeks in his class. How many times did he find cause to banish me from the room, to stand outside in the porch, often with feelings of puzzled bewilderment at such treatment? Consequently, it was not long before I found excuses to be absent from school, long periods being spent working on the farm, which resulted in sporadic visits and increasing threats from the truant officer.

This early failing in my education was replaced by the welcome substitute of learning the ways of the countryside. With lessons over for the day we would be released from the little chapel school to make our way home along the old and picturesque lane. The collecting of rabbit food picked from the hedgerows on this homeward trek was always a pleasure, culminating in the delight of feeding the dozen or so rabbits that the old man kept. We would fly in through the gate with armfuls of hog weed and open the rickety home-made cages, stuffing handfuls into each, while fussing the furry residents with great affection. The pride of this collection of animals was a pedigree Belgium hare that the old countryman had won several prizes with at the fur and feather club of which he was a member.

It was amusing to watch him and my mother walk down the path and out of the gate on their way to those club meetings, held in the village. They would waddle off up the lane, arm in arm, she pigeon-toed, her feet veering inward, he with flat feet sticking out. Their four sons would be left to find their own amusement, sawing wood, gardening or, sometimes during the late summer months, blackberrying. What joy we would find in racing out across the meadows clutching our odd collection of tin containers, the plump berries that weighed down the hedgerows soon staining our hands as we filled our pots. We rashly ignored the razor-sharp thorns that scored our arms and the biting nettles that brushed our bare legs, as we foraged deep in the folds of those fruit-laden bushes.

It was a boyish bravery that was one day to prove a harsh lesson to Billy – for ever after a reminder of the foolishness of such careless behaviour. There he was, wedged securely in the thickest brambles, merrily harvesting the scores of berries. He lingered in that same position, not heeding the nettles that viciously stung his skinny pink legs. Soon, it seems, the persistent smarting had grown too painful to bear. He stepped out from the blackberry bush, peering down as he did so, to examine those tender limbs. It was at that moment, with his head still bowed low, that he let out a series of terrified screams.

"Aaargh! Aaargh! Help me! Ouch! Help me!" he cried. "Get 'em off me! They're stingin' me legs!"

We peered out with alarm from the bush where we worked, to watch, in a sort of stunned amazement, the little lad leaping up and down on the greensward like a May reveller.

It seems that, unwittingly, he had been standing on a particularly lively red ants' nest. The enraged insects had swarmed up his legs, giving the appearance of a pair of scarlet socks that came up above his knees to almost touch the hem of his short trousers, hundreds and thousands of the vicious creatures violently biting the invading flesh.

Happily, he suffered no more than a serious rash, and that had disappeared in a few days. But never again did he loiter long in a hedge when out blackberrying.

The picking of fruit from our small orchard was never a chore we shirked. For among the half a dozen trees in our garden was a greengage with the most delicious fruit I have ever tasted. My mother would make jams, pickles and pies with all that could be harvested in the season. We would shin up the tree and for every four or five greengages collected, the ripest and juiciest would be selected and eaten there and then.

It was not unusual to be enjoying this stored assortment of pickles and jams as far away as Christmas and beyond. How much more simple, how necessarily basic, the Yuletide season was in those childhood years. Christmas week would see my mother busy in the kitchen mixing the ingredients of the plum pudding in a great earthenware bowl, her four young boys peering into the fruit-laden vessel with radiant smiles.

"Can we have a stir, Mum?" the youngest would whine, stretching his head up to observe her reaction.

"Yes dear, you can all have a stir," she would reply tenderly, her face glowing from the heat of the oven. "And make a wish on the third stir," she would add.

"You gonna put a sixpence in this one, Mum?" the little one would continue.

We each took our turn closing our eyes and making a wish as we stirred, the lookers-on catching a glimpse of the silver sixpence as it surfaced momentarily, then disappeared as fast again back into the mixture.

Christmas Eve would pass much as any other day, except for a noticeable increase in the amount of cooking taking place in the kitchen. We would be upstairs and in bed extra early, four socks hanging at the end of our old iron beds. By morning the four large socks, which belonged to the old man, would be bulging full with apples, oranges, nuts and perhaps a banana or two. Downstairs there were few presents to excite us, Old Harry's meagre wages not stretching to such luxuries. A blank-paged drawing book and an assortment of crayons was perhaps my most memorable present.

Occupying my mind by learning to sketch, with studies of the ornaments in the room, portraits of the family or, sometimes, an imaginary landscape of the countryside, gave me endless hours of quiet pleasure.

The high point of the day was always Christmas dinner, consisting each year of a joint of meat, a gift from the farmer. The remainder of the day would be spent drawing, or reading quietly, the old man sitting in his Windsor chair gazing vacantly into the fire, while puffing his pipe with a noticeable contentment.

His habitual smoking was his only vice, for he rarely went to the pub and over the Christmas period never touched a drink. His wife too was teetotal, although at Christmas time she would make an exception and delicately sip a tot or two of sherry, her little finger protruding as she held the glass, as if an essential guide to the whole performance.

The old farmer of Swallows Farm no doubt enjoyed his Yuletide drink too, for earlier in the year he would ask Harry's children to go out to the fields and pick dandelions to make wine. We would be paid a few shillings for this task.

This job, although backbreaking, was not nearly as demanding as hoeing. How painful my back then, thinning beet in the field all day and agonising to keep up with the more experienced labourers who worked beside me. But those few odd hours or occasional days I spent employed on the farm in my childhood years are filled with fond memories. It was, as I look back, a privilege to have witnessed the passing of that old way of life.

5 Selling Flowers by the Roadside

Old Harry's work at Swallows Farm came abruptly to an end around the second year we were with him, and with unemployment came the inevitable hardships. The good relationship with the farmer was irrevocably severed, to a point at which the old man was under constant threat of eviction for the several months it took him to find another place of employment.

Money coming into the house was so low during this lean time that the old countryman found he was unable to even afford to buy tobacco on many occasions.

"Come on you boys," he would plead in his worst craving moments! "Can't you go out and find us some dog-ends to smoke?"

We would pick up his tobacco tin and wander out along the country lanes and main roads in search of those craved-for cigarette ends. Often we would loiter outside the village pub, finding there a sufficient number to almost fill the tin. With this treasured haul we would amble off up the road, peeling the papers from the dry, stale and foul-smelling tobacco.

The strange novelty that we found in this base scheme swiftly wore off after two or three excursions, so we soon looked for a diversion.

"See who can collect the most of these!" chuckled my step-brother Jim, as he stooped to pick up a discarded cigarette packet. He held it aloft. "Bet I find more'n you anyways!"

We all rose to the challenge, combining 'dog-end hunting', with 'cigarette packet collecting'.

"Hey, what about this one?" we would shout on finding an unusual packet. It was soon added to the growing collection, which included such names as Navy Cut, Strand, Silk Cut, Piccadilly, Marlborough, Woodbine, Craven A, Turf, Park Drive and many other brands, a large number of which no longer exist.

One day we set off across the fields, making a beeline for the main road in our hunt for those addictive dog ends. The path led through an ancient section of woodland, where shortly we came to an opening in the canopy. Here the sun came through and saturated an expanse of lush green moss, with here and there carpets of violets and primroses. The sweet scent from this profusion of woodland flowers hung heavy in the morning air, and we lingered a while, the youngest child amusing himself by picking his mother a bouquet of violets.

Tony, always the first to dream up a scheme to earn a penny or two, came up with the idea of selling bunches of these flowers. "Coo, yeah, what a great idea!" Jim shouted, his face lighting up with an eager grin. "We could sell 'em up in the London markets!"

"Don't be silly Jim! How we gonna get up there?" burst out Tony, instantly checking the lad's over enthusiasm. "No!" he continued. "We'll sell 'em here! Out on the road!"

We each harvested as great a variety as we could carry. Then, laden to the hilt, we wandered out to the main road – four country waifs, each holding up a bunch of violets and primroses to the passing traffic that in those days was scarcely more than one car every ten to fifteen minutes. Our first and only customer drew up past us slowly, came to a halt, then reversed. It was a young couple, a woman in the passenger seat, a fair and pretty lady. She smiled sweetly as she wound down the window.

"Are they for sale?" she asked, her blue eyes wondering over the array of flowers we held.

"Yes Ma'am," I replied nervously. Then continued as an afterthought, "They're fruppence a bunch!"

A slender white hand reached out of the car window and she passed me a silver florin, then took a variety of both primroses and violets.

With the car disappearing up the road, we scampered back across the fields clutching the remaining posies, all thoughts of selling more flowers that day gone. The two shillings, we reasoned, was more than ample to keep us in sweets for ages.

It was not long after this that the old man found another place of employment, the job being in the Lewes area of East Sussex, at Upper Clay Hill Farm, three miles from Ringmer. His new employer sent him down an old cattle truck to use as a removal van. It had been thoroughly washed out, yet still reeked strongly of cow manure but served the purpose, holding all our furniture with room to spare.

6 The Return to Dial Post

It was a chill February afternoon when, a little over half a century later, I returned to Dial Post to see again that quaint cottage that was once my childhood home. The village appeared to have come through the years with only minor changes. The old 'chapel school' had sadly gone, replaced by a group of ugly, red brick bungalows. Swallows Lane, I was heartened to see, remained unaltered. The broad-leafed trees, dotted here and there among the bulky hedgerows that flanked the road, looked as pretty as ever. There too, close by the entrance to Swallows Farm, was the tiny strip of copse land, forever a cool shade to pass through on hot summer days.

As luck would have it, the cottager who now occupied Cherry Tree Cottage was busy pottering about the garden when I drew up to the place. The stocky, grey-haired figure looked up, a little startled at my sudden appearance at her garden gate.

"Hi!" I said, with a broad smile, eager to put her at ease. "I used to live here! My old step dad, Harry Pateman, worked up at the farm back in the fifties."

"Oh, yes!" she replied, with an unsure smile. Then gathering her thoughts she continued, "Yes! Yes! I do remember the name."

She then went on to explain that she was the wife of the farmer, Mr. Sawyer, who had retired several years ago. They had given up the farm, moved out of the great farmhouse and into the cottage.

"The old place still looks much as it did when I lived there," I said cheerfully.

"Yes," she replied frowning, "but the farm isn't the same as it used to be."

"Oh, why is that then?" I prompted.

"Well, some of the barns are now used as industrial units."

"Regrettably, that's often the way nowadays," I pointed out.

"I know," she continued. "And all the fields over the back of the house are fenced in with high wire mesh."

"That's a shame," I said. "We used to pick primroses and violets in the wood over the back, and sell them out on the road you know."

"You wouldn't now," she added in her deep Sussex tongue; her expression showing much disapproval at the locking in of the land. "It's highly private over there these days."

Her face darkened still more as she cast a glance over the weed-infested fields that lay to the front of the cottage.

"Look at that lot," she said with a note of despair. "There's over five hundred acres out there. All going to waste. While thousands of people are starving in the world. And why? For money, that's why. It pays more to leave the fields barren than to cultivate them."

My eyes took in the sorry sight. For there, where once the fields were full of wheat, was now no more than a plantation of docks, bindweed and umpteen other wasteland plants.

There was little more to say. I bid my farewells and wandered off up the lane, my thoughts dwelling much on how I longed to roam again, through fields of swaying corn, three brothers by my side.

7 Clay Hill Farm, Ringmer

The tied cottage at Upper Clay Hill lay beside the road, on the brow of a hill. It had a plain, modern appearance and was one of a pair built specifically for farm workers. Franz, our neighbour, was the head cowman. He was a German, an ex-P.O.W, who had settled down in this country after the war and married an English girl. They had a family of four young children, ranging from seven to a year old.

We soon settled in, and within a week my brothers and I were sent to our new school, a large Victorian building in Ringmer, almost three miles from the house where we lived. The old man was still feeling the pinch for money some few weeks after the move, so we were packed off to school each morning with a couple of jam sandwiches, which was all my mother could afford for our midday meal.

The trudge there each morning was, in spite of the distance, nothing for four healthy boys who could find plenty of amusement on the journey. Our only misery was having to leave the house with little food in our bellies, and that often resulted in eating our sandwiches en route.

The one other discomfort was discovered the second week we were there. It was a filthy, wet and windy morning when we set off from the house, my mother having great reservations at having to send us out in such weather. With the rain beating full into our faces, we bent our heads to the wind and kept going. By the first mile we were drenched to the skin, our short coats having no effect in keeping the weather out. On reaching school, we fell in line with the village children who hastily filed into the cloakroom, their hats and coats barely damp, having run between the spots in the short dash from their homes.

My brothers dragged their saturated forms to their respective classrooms, while my sodden shoes squelched a route to my desk, where I sat, shivering and dripping sizeable puddles on the classroom floor. The auburn haired teacher studied me for some minutes, looking distressed at the sight of the wretched child before her.

"Have you not got wellingtons to wear in this weather?" she asked.

"No miss," I replied miserably.

"Well, where's your overcoat?" she said, with noticeable concern.

"Haven't got one Miss!" I mumbled.

She pondered over the situation momentarily.

"Well, you had better move your desk over by the fire and dry off then."

The coal-burning stove stood in the far corner of the room, its tubular asbestos chimney reaching up and out through the roof. I glanced over to it, then back to her, nodding as I did so in eager acceptance of the idea. I very soon dragged my desk to within half a foot of the burner. And as the day wore on, my soaking clothes steamed, dried, and I warmed like toast – and there, beside the radiant heat, remained my desk for the duration of the time I was at that school.

As I was a new pupil, thrown into the school during the mid-term session, the head teachers had, from the outset, to assess my level of academic learning. During this period of processing I was placed in the bottom of the lowest class, which gave rise to the notion that I was being held back, as if a poor, difficult scholar. These general guidelines adhered to by academic establishments, were to hinder my learning throughout my schooldays, for I never did reach a very high standard. The crux of the problem was, without doubt, our frequent shuffling from pillar to post, moving from one new school to another.

So it was, that on that filthy wet morning, in the old school at Ringmer, that I first became aware of this failure in my education. The idea had sunk in, and remained in my mind all day and into the afternoon, and there it stayed throughout the long trek home. The return journey on those cold, wet and miserable days always seemed drearier than the setting off in the morning. Perhaps it was that, in spite of the fire we kept burning in the house, the place never felt warm, never inviting.

Our fuel was the dead wood we gathered and carried home from a hazel copse a quarter of a mile away. We would tie great bundles with binding string, then throw them over our shoulders and stagger back up the hill to home. This heavy task did not last long though, for in clearing brambles at the far end of the garden we uncovered an old dump where previous occupiers had thrown their unwanted goods. Among the rubbish we discovered an old rusting pram that we soon converted into a box cart. The newly acquired trolley gave the wood-collecting expeditions a more inspired and exciting edge.

From our house at the top of the hill we would take turns riding down the steep slope, two at a time. The remaining brothers would give the truck a hefty push, sending us off with boyish shouts of delight, the cart always gathering sufficient speed in its downward flight to almost reach the hazel copse. The old pram would again be laden to the hilt with wood and hauled back up the hill, with excited chatter and friendly arguments about whose turn it was to take the next thrilling ride on the return trip.

This few acres of copse land soon became our regular haunt, where besides gathering wood we spent hours of idle amusement. Bird-nesting was always a favourite, though sometimes we would search for hazel saplings suitable for making bows and arrows. Once selected, these slender, willowy rods were artistically shaved of their bark then looped with binding string to make what we considered powerful longbows. Brotherly competitions were the first test of our efforts, to see whose arrow was propelled the furthest or was the more accurate.

While roaming about this patch of woodland one day, I noticed a small hole at eye level in a tree. I carelessly stuffed my hand into the cavity and prodded about in search of a nest. Finding nothing there, I reached up to where the tips of my fingers came in contact with a velvety coated creature that I could not identify by touch. Withdrawing my hand sharply, I peered in and could just make out the dark shape of a noctule bat, suspended from a ledge. Cupping the little chap in my hand, I gently unhooked his feet and brought him out to the sunlight. It was a novel feeling. How exciting, I thought, to have the opportunity to handle an animal that I had previously only wondered at as it fluttered about the barns and outbuildings around the farm, its flight so swift, its form so elusive in the dusky light of evening. Yet there it was, nestled in my hand, unruffled by my attention, my touch – my earliest studies into the fascinating world of this wild creature of the night.

"Is he alive?" asked Jim, the older step-brother.

"Yeah, I think so," I said, as I passed the tiny nocturnal beast to him.

"Best put him back. Don't want him dying like that owl," piped up Billy, referring to a baby owl we had found a day or two before. We had brought the tiny chick home with the idea of feeding and taming it for a pet, but it had died overnight.

I carefully replaced the motionless bat on his secluded perch and we headed off up the hill to home. On entering the garden gate, my eyes wandered over to the clear view of the South Downs, no more than three or four miles away.

How many times had I gazed from our garden in wonder at those smooth, enticing hills, my youthful mind conjuring up volumes of adventures that might be had in so distant and seemingly prohibited a world. The soft curves, the irregular mounds, those mysterious sunken paths, together aroused my curiosity to such an extent that the temptation to visit them became too great. Several times I put the idea of going there to my brothers, but they had no interest in making such a trip.

"No Dave," they would say. "We ain't gonna walk that far! And anyway, the old man will go mad if he finds out."

So it was that within the first few weeks of living at Clay Hill

I took it into my head to walk alone to those mysterious hills. Setting off as early as I dared, and telling only my elder brother Tony, I walked the four miles to the foot of Malling Down.

How awesome that hill appeared as I drew up to it and began climbing! The turf underfoot was soft and springy, and I fair bounded up the steep slope, higher and higher, the warm, late spring air feeling cooler as I neared the summit. I paused to look round, and there before me was the grandest, most exhilarating view I had ever seen. I looked on spellbound.

"Wow!" burst from my lips. "Wowee!" I cried again, overcome with excitement. Then I turned on my heels and sped away, further and further up and over those smooth, graceful hills, gleefully hollering "Wheyee! Wheyeee!" as I went.

On and up I scampered, the great expanse of those downs fuelling an intense feeling of freedom that spurred me on until I finally reached the highest point of Mount Caburn, where I collapsed and rolled over on my back exhausted, breathless. How long I lay there will always be a mystery: time was meaningless. I gazed up at the white sailing clouds, the deep blue sky beyond, my heaving chest slowing to a more even pace, the sweet scent of thyme reaching my nostrils with every breath. There I bathed in the warm sunshine, and listened for ages to the hum of bees, their incessant buzzing adding eerily to the solitude.

It was some long time before I stirred from my idle daydreams. I stood up and wandered a haphazard path down the hill, a clear, cool southerly breeze brushed my face in my steady progress. Far below, I could see the old town of Lewes, that looked for all the world like a tiny Lilliputian hamlet, with the River Ouse snaking a course through the lower quarter.

I gawped in wonder at the novel scene, but my euphoria was soon interrupted by the unmistakable clamour of jackdaws. Quite suddenly I had come to the edge of a chalk quarry, with a sheer drop of three or four hundred feet. I stood transfixed. The very steepness of the cliff, the great gap of open space, was awesome.

The squabbling birds again drew my childish attention. I stood watching them for some time, fascinated by their antics. They would land precariously on a narrow ledge close by their nest holes, fidget their feet and look here and there like nervous clerics before entering their dark chambers. I lay down on my belly on the soft downy turf and rested my head in cupped hands, lazily watching the comical stunts of those black-coated daws. The afternoon sun drifted low, appearing watery with misty hues of yellow, warning me that I soon had to leave. The journey home was long and tiresome, and dusk had fallen damp and uncomfortable when I walked in the door.

Little more than a week later, I found myself back on the chalk cliff with my brothers, looking again down on the old town of Lewes. The prospect of getting an egg or two had proved too great a temptation when I told them of the nesting daws. An old rick rope had been discreetly borrowed from the farm for the purpose, and we stood there craning our necks over the precipice in search of the easiest way to get our prize.

"Hey! Let's tie the rope on that post over there, and lower one of us down to that nest hole," I said, pointing to a stake some twenty feet away, that was part of the safety fence at the top of the quarry. All agreeing it was a good idea, we lashed the cord to the selected post, between us half hinting that Billy should be the one to go down the cliff.

"I'm not going down there!" he whimpered.

"Why not? You're the lightest," reasoned Jim.

"Yer! And you're a far better climber than any of us," added Tony, with a devilish grin.

"I can't! What if I fall?" whined the now worried looking child.

"You won't fall Billy! We'll tie the rope on you, and lower ya down gently," I said, demonstrating my meaning by slipping the rick rope under his arms and tying a knot.

"No! No! I don't want to!" he pleaded, as we edged him towards the sheer drop.

"Come on Billy! You can do it! You only gotta go down to that hole there, put your hand in and get an egg," persuaded Tony, helping the terrified lad over the cliff, his hands and feet desperately searching for safe holds as he descended. A newly discovered bravery was now apparent in his daring attitude.

"See if you can get over to that nest hole," called out Tony, pointing to a cavity a few feet to the right of his plucky brother, who had climbed sufficiently down to be in line with the hole indicated.

He gingerly moved a foot to the right, dislodging a loose chip of malm stone as he did so. Panic took grip, and his feet scrambled for a foothold sending a small avalanche of chalk shards into the three hundred foot chasm. The rope pulled heavily and the brave little lad swung to and fro in the great void, like the pendulum of a clock. We all looked on in horror.

"Hold on Billy! We'll pull you up," I bellowed, as we all tugged at the life saving cord. Soon the hero appeared, his face white, his eyes wide, the look of terror spread across his features. We grasped his shaking arms and hauled him to the safety of the firm turf, all declaring as we did so, that it would be impossible to climb down to get those jackdaw eggs.

8 Black Tea in the Cornfields

The months rolled on, and before we knew it school holidays had begun and the harvest was in full swing. We had set off in the morning to help on the farm and as time drew on it turned out to be one of those sweltering hot days, the kind that saps the strength of all living creatures. Yet there we were, four brothers and the countryman, brown as berries in the cornfield laboriously stooking corn. We slowly followed the binder that chattered a methodical course round the field, the whole scene a picture that might easily have graced the canvas of any artist a hundred years before.

The afternoon sun scorched down on my back, my arms raw with the incessant scratching of dried thistle wrapped up in the sheaves. I paused to examine the inflamed sores, plucking from each limb half a dozen or more bristle-like thorns, then wandered to the far side of the shimmering field where a cool drink lay stored under the shade of a stook. It was cold black tea, and I guzzled it greedily as a child will, throwing back my head to tilt the bottle almost vertical, my eyes piercing the deep blue sky. It was then that I noticed a few odd segments of straw floating down from that infinite blue. I was amazed, and I watched in wonder, trying to discover how it came about.

With my hands shielding my squinted eyes from the glare of the sun, I searched the expanse of stubble land but could see nothing to explain such a strange phenomenon. I looked again, swivelling my head full round, and this time I noticed, several hundred yards away, a flurry of stray straws missed by the sails of the binder. They were being sucked up by the warm thermals, as if caught by a mini whirlwind, to circle high in the vortex and finally descend some distance to another part of the field. I hurried over to my brothers, pointing out my discovery, and they looked on fascinated.

The afternoon wore on and the ever-chattering machine neared the last cut of the corn, and rabbits scurried in all directions.

"Poor things. Wish we could catch one and take 'im home," said Billy.

His whining caught the ear of Old Harry, who was in the process of tucking a sheaf under each arm.

"You can catch 'em easy, boy! You only gotta put some salt on their tails," he teased with a wry smile.

"Cor! Wish I had some salt, Pop," replied the child, unaware that he was the butt of the old countryman's devilish humour.

We all chuckled at the old man's fun. But the little lad had been fooled more than we had supposed, for we discovered some long time later that for many months he had carried in his pocket a pinch of salt wrapped up in paper especially for the purpose of popping it onto the tails of wild rabbits.

"Fat chance you'll 'ave of getting one with that!" we all laughed when we found him out.

A few weeks later and work was going ahead with the getting in and ricking up of the stooked corn. The old carts, converted from horse-drawn to use for tractor, hitch and tow, would rumble at a snail's pace across the stubble fields and along rutted lanes in a constant flow, feeding the men who built the stacks. It was a pretty sight to see those old wagons laden to the hilt with sheaves sway into the allotted rick yard. My brothers would ride precariously a-top the heaving cart, while I had been singled out to help build the three picturesque circular ricks that resulted from the harvest, the men having the opinion that "one boy's a boy, two boys be half a boy, and three or four boys be no boy at all".

How amusing it was to listen to the ready wit that sprouted from the several farm hands I worked with during those stacking operations. They would keep me in fits of laughter with their jibes.

"Come on, boy, get a move on! You'll 'ave ta get some elbow grease ya' know!" they would chuckle, ribbing me in my struggles with the task of tossing sheaves to them with the pitchfork.

Another time, while finding difficulty stretching over from the rick ladder to the stack, I almost came a cropper, my short legs being the crux of the problem. "The'll have to put some dung in ya boots lad! That'll make ya grow!" they mocked, falling into guffaws of laughter, and putting a lighter note on what could have been a serious accident.

Then again, before the start of work, it had been a particularly dense misty morning. I made a comment on the weather.

"Fog's thick this morning!" I said, as I climbed the rick ladder, addressing my observations to the men above me.

"Thick, cor, that ain't thick!" replied one of them. "Why, when I were a lad, I remember it being so dense you couldn't see nothin' about you at all. Why, that day I recall, even the rooks was walking about the fields and lanes to get to their colony for fear of flying into each other in mid-flight!"

His little story caused some smiles amongst the rustics.

We would often walk round the corn ricks of a morning before the start of work, searching for the tiny harvest mice that were carried in from the fields in the sheaves. It was not unusual to find a dozen or more as they scurried about the unfinished stacks. They were docile little things, appearing almost tame as they ran up and down our arms to our great amusement. At one time we took three or four home to make pets of them, but first one died, then a few days later another, until we lost them all. Stepbrother Jim was so taken by the red tint of their coats that he skinned them as they died

'There we were, four brothers and the countryman, brown as berries in the cornfield, laboriously stooking corn.' Clockwise from top left: Harry, Jimmy, David, Tony and Billy

and nailed their pelts, stretched and salted, on the shed door. What became of the cured furs I know not. The idea of treating those dead animals in such a way disgusted me, and I turned my back on the scheme, preferring instead to lose myself in my then newly-discovered hobby of clay modelling.

There was an abundance of the pliant material in the garden, and I found great pleasure in moulding oddly shaped pots, bowls or any curious figures that came to mind. My childish efforts with pottery were not destined to last long though, for there was no way of firing the pieces produced, so in time they returned to the earth from whence they came. For me, it was one of those periods in my childhood when everything was of interest. I wanted to know, investigate and delve into the ways and means of all that existed.

On one occasion, when my mother had gone to Lewes for some shopping, I took the opportunity to discover how to make leaden objects. The clay in the garden I used as a mould, impressing interesting shapes into the malleable casts. The lead was more difficult to come by, beyond the scheme I had of using the few base metal toys I possessed that had been picked up for a penny or two from jumble sales by my mother. I reasoned with the idea of the old man finding out, and the consequence of what would happen if he discovered my scheme.

"He'll never find out," I concluded, resolute to carry through the project no matter what.

I charged upstairs to my room and selected the largest lead item I could find amongst my scarce selection of toys. It was a battered, gold coloured coronation coach and horses.

With Old Harry at work, I knew it would be safe to have a small bonfire at the end of the garden for the purpose of melting the lead. Time and again I tried to get the kindling to catch fire, but it was far too damp. Not to be beaten, I rummaged in the shed for a can of oil that I had discovered some while back. There it was, still sitting in the corner, covered in cobwebs: it had been left there, forgotten by the previous tenants. I brushed the grime off the lid and prised it open with the sharp end of the anvil. An inch or two of thick, dark oil lay in the bottom of the two-gallon container.

"That'll do to get the twigs to burn," I imagined.

With a few fresh sheets of crumpled newspaper shoved under the brushwood I touched a match to it and flames licked up through the saturated pile, turning the wood black. I tilted the rusting can to feed the fire. The glowing heat came in contact with the inflammable liquid, and in that instant there was a blinding flash, a spontaneous explosion, and the can shot like a rocket out of my hands and across the garden.

Our old dog Judy, who had been sniffing round my heels at the time, was so frightened that she leapt about three feet in the air, bolted across the vegetable plot and through a hole in the hedge, where beyond grazed the dairy cows. I stood on the spot, shaking but happily not burnt. It was obvious that a splash or two of petrol had been mixed with the oil, the fumes instantly igniting.

Within a few minutes the old dog skulked back to the garden, its tail between its legs. I peered over the hedge a little concerned. There, as suspected, I noticed that the cows had taken fright and were careering across the meadow. The farmer in the distance looked on.

"He's too far away to have seen, or heard anything," I reasoned, and so resumed my task of lighting the bonfire. It took a while, but did eventually flare up, with flames licking round the base of an old saucepan, in which was placed the lead article. The heat was fierce, and it was not long before it took effect, with the lower portions of the soft metal soon turning liquid. I watched with the anticipation of an excited scientist, and there observed with immense satisfaction the complete coronation coach and horses dissolve to molten lead. I was unaware that in time this very piece would become highly collectable and worth several hundreds of pounds, but the experiment was to some extent a success, in that I discovered some primitive methods of moulding lead.

That evening, the old man came home from work, his spirits a little higher than was usual after a day's toil.

"The guvnor's a funny old sod!" he chuckled as he came in through the back door.

"How's that then dear?" asked my mother, with an inquisitive frown.

"Well, he reckons the boys have been over here setting off fireworks!" he replied "Sez he was out in the back field when one went off! Frightened the cows, he reckoned."

"Well! I've been shopping in Lewes with the boys. The only one at home was David," she said, looking mystified.

"Yes! Well I damn well told 'im. Fireworks, I said. Fireworks! It's the middle of May. Gawd lummy, you don't get fireworks in May! Believe me, Nell. He didn't know what to say after that! It soon shut 'im up!"

The conversation then turned to another topic, while I slunk off to the other room, doing my best to conceal the smirk on my face.

9 A Ghostly Visit

My concern in keeping the lead-making scheme from Harry was due to his somewhat erratic temper, which would erupt with the merest hint of annoyance. He was, there is no doubt, a good man by heart and by nature. Yet a lifetime of toil, with little or no reward, along with the sporadic periods of unemployment that always resulted in living on the bread line, often terminated in debt and desperation. This way of life eventually took its toll, and he became disagreeable and quick-tempered. So it was that we all learnt to guard our tongues and watch our behaviour when he was around. In spite of this, we all at some time or another fell foul of his low moods, and the consequences were often swiftly dealt with, as was the case not long after my lead-melting experiments.

It had been a wet couple of weeks. The ground was unpleasant and boggy, and my feet stuck fast in the heavy clay as I made my way across the field from our house to the farm. I struggled to pull them free, and then kept going, with splashes of mud covering my legs and plastering the white, enamel milk can I carried in my errand of taking the old man his afternoon tea. He was in the cow shed with our next door neighbour – both dairymen busy with the hand milking.

"Hi ya, Pop! Brought your tea over for you," I chirped in cheerful mood, as I came into the cow-stall. He raised his head from the flank of the cow and peered over to me, his eyes dark and hollow.

"Bloody good mess, ain't it?" he rasped as he snatched the can from me to examine the mud-splattered white container at close range.

"I'm not drinking that tea!" he raged. "So you can take the damn can home again. Look at it! It's covered in filth."

His work companion, Franz, the head cowman, looked up in surprise at the old man's anger and tried to calm matters by pointing out in his broken English that, "Ze tea must be drinkable, as ze milk can has ze vell-made lid zat covers ze contents perfectly."

"That's not the point," the old man raved, his face puffed up, red and boiling. "How'd you manage to git it in such a filthy mess as that?"

My answer was slow and nervously hesitant. The sympathetic head cowman interrupted.

"Hey! Let ze lad be, Harry," he said, in trying to calm the man. "He is only a little vun, and bezides, you know zat field's in ze hell of ze mess."

With this the old man lowered his voice and growled, "Go on! Git off home, and take the filthy tea can with ya!"

I slunk out of the cow shed and back across the field to home.

It had just turned six that evening, and I was busy stacking firewood in the hallway by our back door, when the old man, having finished work, came into the garden and stormed up the path.

"What's the meaning of bringing my tea over in that mud-ridden mess?" he bellowed.

I looked up in alarm and caught the flame in his eye as he bore down on me with an arm outstretched, the other raised threateningly. Ducking down, I dodged through our back door, but he was on me before I could get further. I tripped on the wood pile and fell heavily onto the bottom step of the stairs. My mother dashed through from the sitting room to see what the ruckus was, but there was nothing she could do. The old man, in a moment, snatched up a hefty stick from the log pile and rained blows down on me. I hollered out in terror, then found my feet and bolted up the stairs, while Harry, not caring to make the flight with me, remained where he was and all went quiet. I lay on my bed until sleep carried me through to the following morning. With a fresh day, the whole episode of the evening before was of no great consequence.

It was no more than a few weeks later when, in succession, we all went down with a heavy dose of flu. Asian flu, they said; but, whatever the strain, it was sufficiently vicious to lay each one of us out for several weeks. Even my mother's usual resilience against such infections proved of no help. There we lay, each one of us in a shivering sweat, our boiling heads tossing and perspiring on soaking pillows – forever restless, burning up with the virulent fever for a fortnight and more – while the old man went about the house, seemingly impervious to the highly-infectious disease.

With our slow recovery there emerged the possible answer to the old man's immunity. He had, it seems, eaten, as was his habit, a raw onion every day to ward off the infection. This remedy we had always scoffed at, but he would have it that such things worked.

"To fend off coughs and colds," he would point out in defence.

At least once a week he would wander in from the garden peeling a juicy, plump onion, freshly plucked from the vegetable plot, and sink his bulky false teeth into the flesh. There he would stand, munching it like an apple, while those in close vicinity would soon fall victim to the vicious vapours. Eyes would stream as the zesty flavours radiated about the room, while he appeared impervious to the hot and violent fumes.

He was, there is no doubt, a hardy countryman, a man of strong constitution. Yet, at the same time, there was a certain softness about his character, for he could not bear to see any form of cruelty to animals. How greatly he cared for our cats, my mother's endearing pets! We had at one time as many as half a dozen, each one of which he fussed with enormous affection. Whenever they prowled round the corner of the house and trotted up to him, to rub their noses over his muddy boots, he would stoop and stroke them with the gentle care of a child.

Strangely, the cats were one day the cause of several months of misery. It came about one late afternoon, when Harry trudged home across the field at the end of his day's work. He wearily climbed the stile at the foot of our garden, then wandered up the path. Before he could reach the back door he was confronted by our neighbour, Franz, who glared over from his patch of ground.

"You vill have to keep your vilthy cats under betta control Harry!" he bawled over to him angrily. "Zey are alvays over here, scratching an' doing zer stinking mess in my garden vere my kids have to play."

The old man stood stock still, a look of disbelief on his face at being spoken to in such a way. My brothers and I were busy with our chore of unloading kindling from the cart. We looked up in bemused amazement, while old Harry reared up in anger and bellowed back with some force that he had "never seen his cats going over to their garden to do their business".

"Vell, I am telling you zat they have!" the furious neighbour raged, striding menacingly towards Harry, who was unable to avoid the man, there being no dividing fence between the two plots.

The old countryman stood his ground as a further volley of words were exchanged, and then in an instant fists were flying in all directions. We looked on desperately as, to our horror, the dairyman Franz turned briefly to grab a garden spade that rested against the shed wall and swung it heavily. The old man's face contorted in agony as the iron implement crashed into his stomach, another swing bent him double. He fell and rolled over writhing with pain on the path.

The whole affray was over in a few minutes, but in that time the old countryman was badly injured, having suffered much bruising about the face and a couple of broken ribs. He was off work for several months to allow his damaged bones to heal, gathering strength in the process for his return to work. During this lengthy period of convalescence he had uncharacteristically developed an intense dislike for Germans, the like of which was not before apparent. We would often catch him as he wandered about the house muttering under his breath, "Bloody Germans, there never was a good 'un."

At other times he would raise himself awkwardly from his old armchair, or drop heavily down on the seat by the dining table, groaning as he did so, "Oh mother, me side do 'urt." Then again he would get up and shuffle out to another room, mumbling as he went, "Bugger the bloody German, there never was a good 'un."

The rift between the two neighbours did, however, eventually improve to a respectful nod, or a muttered "morning" in the comings and goings of each day. The old man had decided to drop all assault charges, and they were on talking terms by the time he got back to his job, though never to the close friendliness that had existed before.

Old Harry had not been back at work for more than a week or two before both households experienced a most uncanny phenomenon. The day had been typical of early autumn, damp, chill and overcast, though clearing to a brighter afternoon. We had gone to our bedrooms, the break in the weather having come too late for any outdoor amusement, and besides, the old man expected his children to be asleep by seven thirty most nights.

The light was falling fast and we lay on our beds, still fully dressed, straining our eyes to read in the ensuing dusk. All was silent apart from the occasional, irritating snuffle, snort or cough that was always apparent with my brothers in their moments of concentration. Suddenly, that studious quiet was broken by Harry, bellowing up to us, demanding that we get to bed and stop hanging things out the window. We all looked up from our books, puzzled by his accusation and shouted back down to him almost in chorus, "We ain't doing nothing, Pop! We're reading."

"Well one of you are!" he bawled back.

We were a little bemused when he told us that he and my mother had seen something distinctly white prowl by the sitting room window.

"Well it was nothing to do with us," we protested.

"Then it must be them kids next door playing about," he said angrily from the foot of the stairs. "I'll go round there and soon put a stop to that!"

With this, we watched him from the top of the stairwell stride out through the back door, leaving it fully open as he went. No sooner had he gone than there was a knock on the same rear door, and there stood the dairyman, Franz, his figure a dark silhouette in the door frame. My mother, who had noticed him walk by the front room window, had glided through to greet him.

"Hello Nellie," he said in an almost apologetic voice. "Vought I should let you know your children, zay are playing aboot, hanging zomething white, like a pillowcase, over ze vindow! It upzet ze wife terribly!"

The colour drained a little from Nellie's face as she took in what the man had said. For, as it sank in, she suddenly realised that there might be some greater mystery in the strange event than first supposed. She composed herself, then stoutly defended her four sons by making it clear that they were all "upstairs quietly reading."

"So it must be your children!" she continued. "Harry's just gone round to see you about the same thing. You just missed him. He went round the back as you came round the front of the house. You see, we too saw it in *our* window!"

The now confused neighbour rested an elbow on the door and stood there some while, looking dumbfounded.

"But my children, zay have been asleep zis past hour!" he mumbled. Just then, Harry returned and interrupted the perplexed man, and between them they conferred and prattled way into the evening, but could come to no conclusion as to the cause of so strange an apparition.

The local farming community soon got to hear of the "haunting up at Clay Hill", which gave rise to some interesting stories that it was thought might account for the visiting spectre. One suggestion was that it was the ghost of some young girl that had long ago, in "ye olde coaching days", been killed in an accident on the brow of the hill, beside the house.

Another good candidate was that of the lost and wandering spirits of two 18th-century soldiers. The men had apparently shot each other and died simultaneously in a duel that took place at the entrance to Pashetts Farm, no more than a few fields distant from Clay Hill. Two wooden crosses still mark their graves on the cross-roads of Norlington Lane and Broyle Lane, Ringmer.

Beyond these local legends, no other explanation has been put forward as to what it was that appeared at the windows of both households at precisely the same time. The only real certainty is that the parents of both families were sufficiently disturbed by what they had seen to make a very determined issue of it with their children and respective neighbour, neither being aware of the other's innocence in the mysterious occurrence.

10 Threshing the Corn

The tiny ripple of amusement that the strange haunting had aroused among the local rustics was short lived, for a few weeks later when I was off school, helping with the threshing, there was no mention of the "eerie haunting". Perhaps it was that the men were too busy with the task in hand to bother with such idle tales, the setting up and starting of machinery being a long acquired skill that, if misjudged, could well prove dangerous.

I can picture them now as they swarmed round the old Field Marshall tractor. The engine was proving difficult to start. The usual method of loading a shot-gun type cartridge into the breach of the intake system, then tapping a pin with a hammer to set the charge off, had failed several times. A build up of carbon had jammed the single-cylinder, two-stroke engine. Several cartridges had been fired to start the great lumbering machine, but it still proved cantankerous, and they huffed and swore vehemently in their efforts to get the thing running. Another cartridge was loaded, then one more resounding bang and it finally fired into action – hesitantly at first, then, with uncertain splutters, smoke puffed and billowed from the exhaust, as if clearing its throat.

It soon settled to a more even pace. The men drew back and the driver manipulated the great thumping engine in line with the threshing machine that had arrived a day or two earlier, while others skilfully secured a massive drive belt onto the pulleys of both machines. Once it was in place a lever was pulled, the belt juddered and then picked up speed, instantly throwing the thresher into life. Every cog, gear and wheel raced and whirred, each precisely set for its own particular purpose. The rolling girdle began to wander dangerously from the spinning pulleys, but this was soon put right by the operator, who pressed a bar of blackjack against the rotating belt, the friction melting the tar-like substance on to the heavy canvas band, reinforcing the adhesion to the casters. With this done he looked up, satisfied that all was safe, then nodded to the eager farmer, indicating that we were ready to start. The signal was all that was required to set the men off with yet another day's toil of threshing.

Billows of dust flew up as the drum throbbed into action, the men adopting a sullen, yet determined stance as they began to pitch the sheaves in a clockwork, relentless fashion. The time drew on and the grime grew denser, enveloping the complete apparatus in a mist that stuck to the sweating brows and bare arms of the farm hands. They laboured on, in silent rhythm.

From my position on the rick I eyed the begrimed workers, concluding that the dirtiest, dustiest job was that held by the sack man. He was a hoary, leathery-faced individual with dark matted hair and scruffy appearance: his fusty-coloured coat was torn, and tied up in the middle with binding string. He sporadically raked the chaff from under the machine and took charge of the sacks when they were full. By the end of each day he was always the blackest, his clothes caked the worst, with a thick layer of coarse dust that hung in a cloud where he worked.

The threshing gang, eager to get the job done before nightfall, assumed a greater urgency in their work and by late afternoon the rick had diminished to a couple of layers of sheaves. Two or three men fell away from the group and unrolled a length of chicken wire. They placed it about the perimeter of the stack, then released from a truck half a dozen yapping terriers into the enclosure.

We worked on and soon came to the last course; the final few sheaves were hastily lifted and, as we did so, rats scurried in every direction. All hell broke loose as the dogs bore down on the petrified rodents that sprang in a crazed frenzy when caught in the wire barrier. Several farm hands leapt in with hefty sticks to help with the slaughter, beating the hideous creatures in mid flight, as a baseball player will hit a ball. Both man and terrier, roused to full-blooded murderous sport, appeared to relish the barbarous annihilation of those terrified brutes.

"Cor! Look at the size of that one," bawled out one excited man.

"Blimey! Mind they don't jump for yer throat, they'll do that when trapped yer know!" shouted another.

"Mind that big bugger over there!" bellowed yet another, as he leapt over to beat the beast down.

And so the rowdy gang carried on, the bloody killing a welcome break in the monotonous toil of threshing. The last sheaf was tossed up and swallowed by the massive thrashing drum and the engine was swiftly cut. All fell suddenly quiet, although seven hours of throbbing, confused noise continued to hum in the ear, heightened the more by the instant silence.

The old farmer, with beaming face, was well pleased with the job done, and equally so with the bloodied heap of dead vermin. He thanked his men heartily and with the sound of the pulsing machine still reeling in my head, I dragged my feet along the darkening lane, the flickering light in our window a few fields away showing my destination.

11 The Floods Are Up

That winter was one of almost perpetual rain, so wet in fact that the River Ouse eventually burst its banks, flooding a number of low-lying fields that belonged to the farm. The water came up over night, and for Harry's four boys it was the sudden arrival of a whole new place of adventure, heralding exciting ideas that could be put to use during the brief existence of those new-born lakes.

Building a raft was the prime suggestion. The scheme, we reasoned, would be easy, for the water had spread up a long, low field and lapped the edge of the higher ground that was the copse where we carried out our daily woodcart trips. We soon got busy with the idea, lopping half a dozen sturdy hazel saplings and trimming them to straight poles, then hauling the product of our labours to the flood line, where we bound them with binding string to form a platform. This done, we launched the craft with great expectations. Our youngest brother, Billy, being the lightest, was hailed by all as captain and briskly put aboard. His delight at being chosen for such a position was, to our regret and his misery, short lived, for no sooner had he clambered on board the vessel than it sank, soaking his socks, shoes and the very fringe of his short trousers.

"Need to cut down more wood and tie it on to make it float better," said Tony, with a note of authority in his voice. We all agreed, and hastily made our way back to the copse where we hacked down another growth of stout hazel rods and lashed them to the raft. But it made no difference: the flimsy platform required much greater buoyancy.

"Think we need some of those old oil drums that's lying about up at the farm," said Tone, "I'll get some tomorrow, when I'm up there helping the old man."

This said, we all put hands to the gunnels and hauled the hulk on to dry land, which is where we found it, still intact, when we returned a couple of days later, laden with our makeshift buoyancy tanks. Strapping them to the clumsy looking contraption we rapidly heaved it into deep water and looked on with pride, but the tubs instantly broke away and bobbed to the surface, like so many buoys in a busy harbour. We then came up with the idea of unhinging the farmer's five-bar gate that divided the field from the copse, and using the wooden barrier to sandwich the oil drums in place on the craft. It worked wonders, and easily took the weight of Billy, who had, with great enthusiasm, been reinstated as captain. He was ready to display his daring, as always, and carelessly punted the raft some good distance across the water while his three elder brothers looked on with apprehension as it drifted further out on the broad floods.

"Don't get out there too far," yelled Tone, but it was too late. We watched in frantic alarm as the vessel was pulled by the swirling waters of the Ouse. The treacherous currents caught hold and raced the helpless craft with its rigid-faced occupant through the violent course of a hundred yards, before miraculously letting go at some unseen deviation in the flow that cast it back to calmer waters. The terrified sailor took no time in cajoling the cumbersome hulk back towards his three gawping brothers, who praised such bravery and leapt aboard as he drew up to them.

The remainder of the day was spent afloat, exploring the full expanse of those temporary lakes, the buoyancy of the home-made raft proving capable of taking the entire weight of four sailing brothers on that voyage of discovery.

A few days later, the floods receded as swiftly as they had arrived. The water had disappeared overnight, leaving the meadows scattered with flotsam that consisted of all kinds of washed-up debris, including the great hulk of our raft that lay in the centre of the field. The farmer, in doing his rounds to survey the flood damage to his land, came across the marooned contraption, noting angrily that it was made up of his copse wood, oil drums and the five-bar gate. It seems he had a fair idea who was responsible, for he made a beeline for old Harry, who tried in vain to defend his boys. But it proved of no use, for he was sacked on the spot and given notice to quit the house, with orders that his four sons were to dismantle the raft and re-hang the gate immediately.

It took very nearly six months for the old man to find another job, during which time we were again reduced to living on the breadline. This rapid decline in our circumstances provoked the old countryman to take extreme measures.

"We'll have to sell what bits we've got about the house, Mother," he announced. "I don't care what it is. We've got to eat! Can't go on without a bit of tommy in our stomachs!"

The old lady, caught unawares by his drastic suggestion, looked up, a fiery flame in her eyes.

"Oh, no Harry, I don't see why we should have to sell up house and home," she grumbled. "And I'm not selling any of my collection of bits."

Her words fell on deaf ears, for the old man won the day. Each morning a few chairs, the table, our sideboard, and a great amount of bric-a-brac and antique artefacts were carted out to the greensward that verged the road. There a 'For Sale' notice was placed conspicuously atop the great jumble of goods to catch the eye of passing traffic. Come evening we would all troop out to the road, to suffer yet again the humiliation of humping the furniture back to the house.

This performance went on day after day, our goods and chattels slowly diminishing as the weeks drew into months. Then, after the passing of half a year, the old man finally secured another job, by which time the rooms were so devoid of furniture that there was a noticeable echo in the house when heavy boots walked over the bare boards. To our embarrassment there were barely sufficient household goods left to warrant the use of the enormous cattle truck that came to collect our belongings. We soon piled these few bits in, then tumbled into the back of the old lorry and rumbled off to our new destination, Lowfold Farm at Wisborough Green.

12 The Return to Ringmer

It was a sweltering hot June day in 2006 when I returned again to Ringmer, to look over my childhood haunts. The old Victorian school had gone, pulled down in 1993. The road through the village was dangerously busy, and I was pleased to get off the route and on to the quieter lane that leads on to Upper Clay Hill.

The cottage where once we had lived, one of a pair, had undergone alterations – knocked into one, with the front garden gate securely blocked by a high, thick-set hedge. The entrance, now at the rear, leads through a small industrial complex, built on ground that was once the green field across which we trekked on our errands to the farm.

How it had all altered in that half century! Far too noisy, I mused, to have a good "haunting" like that in years gone by. No more light could I throw on that strange and spooky happening; no more evidence has come forward relating to that local legend, in which a child is killed in an "olde coaching accident". There was, though, an extra snippet to be had regarding the duelling soldiers buried at the crossroads in Norlington Lane. A diary, written in 1880 by a woman called Nancy Martin, mentions the duel, and it makes interesting reading. Be that as it may, we as a family never did discover the real cause of that spectre-like form that suddenly appeared for a few minutes at our window and our neighbours' at precisely the same time. This perfectly true incident, will, I believe, remain an unexplained mystery.

The farm where Old Harry had worked lay at the end of a short lane, indifferent to the world. Yet, a few years after we had moved, the place was turned into a home of high national security, for none other than James Callaghan, the chancellor of the exchequer, had taken possession of the farm. Later, when he became prime minister, police officers were posted at the gates (due to the troubles in Northern Ireland), making access impossible.

The farmhouse, barns and out-buildings have long since gone out of the honourable gentleman's hands, but there still lingers a very private feeling about the place. It was, for sure, a little disheartening to leave the Ringmer area without having laid my eyes on that old familiar school, the cottage or the farm, as it was in those childhood years.

13 Lowfold Farm

About a mile south of Wisborough Green there nestles Lowfold Farm, remotely situated at the end of a deep rutted lane. Our house, the second one in of a terrace of four, was situated part way along the route and flanked on all sides by dense woodland. Great towering elms and oaks spread their vast canopies over the line of chimneys and dormer windows that protruded quaintly from the tiled roof of the cottages. These broad-leafed trees cast such deep shade over the dwelling during the spring and summer months that the rooms were held in constant darkness. Consequently, studious work was always a strain on eyes, necessitating the daily use of the oil lamp.

Harry's wife soon discovered this inconvenience shortly after moving into the house during the time budding leaves were bursting. Her normally pleasurable pursuit of meticulously stitching the pressed wild flowers she gathered into scrapbooks had become noticeably tedious in the gloomy shadows of the room. Yet in spite of this, there was a sweet homeliness to the place that more than compensated for that lack of light.

Two solid stone steps led up to the front door that opened into a small, but adequate sitting room. Here, there were two doors, one leading out to the tiny kitchen, with its rough masonry sink and stone slabbed floor that was pitted and worn cavernous in places by the incessant scraping of hobnailed boots over the years. The other was the entrance to the stairs, steep, narrow and leading off in a perfect right angle, making the moving in of furniture almost impossible and compelling some pieces to be hoisted up and through the dormer windows.

The two bedrooms were cosy, snug and, uncharacteristically for an old house, warm, no matter what the weather or season. How peaceful it was of an evening to lie resting in bed, the window ajar letting in the fresh night air! The pitch-pipe hoot of the owls would echo through the hollow woodland, reaching the ear with such clarity that it might be thought the bird was no further away than the window ledge.

For me, the most impressionable songster was the nightingale, due, no doubt, to my not being familiar with its song before we came to Lowfold. Throughout the night its fluid notes would drift through the open window in the most melodious ascending scales, delighting the listener with its rich fluting strains that would rise to a clear crescendo, then fall muted and jarring. The whole sequence would be repeated over and over again, but with minute, unexpected alterations. Then, with the twilight of day, its song would be lost in the first notes of the dawn chorus. That would open with the distant song of the thrush, whose mellow throaty voice always seemed a signal for the teasing strains of other woodland birds. The wood warblers would waken with their silvery trills, then the reedy song of the blackcap, while further away the piping whistle of the blackbird filled in the background to a growing tapestry of notes that would soon swell to a festoon of melodious voices pouring forth to reach a resounding intensity. Then, as suddenly as this dawn concert arose, it began to subside, and it was never long before the rising sun flushed the woodland tree tops.

It was in these alluring woods that we would wander in idle moments, or occasionally on our excursions to the nearest shop, a tiny shack-like place situated half a mile as the crow flies, through the dense copseland. Tea, sugar, butter or perhaps the old man's favourite tobacco would be our common quest on those pleasurable missions. We would shuffle in through the door to the cramped porch, where a serving hatch divided the customers from the goods that were stacked in every conceivable space. Here, the rich smell of a multitude of flavours hung in the air as a mouth-watering welcome to its modest number of patrons. The elderly trader would plod through from the shadows of her living room to greet us with a smile that quivered on thin lips.

"Hello boys. What is it you want?" she would say in almost a whisper.

The short list of items was always read out by the eldest of the troop.

"Mum sez can we have an ounce of 'bacca, and half a pound of sugar, please? And we got sixpence to spend between us."

The old storekeeper would mumble as she doddled round to pick out the things requested. She would pop them in a brown paper bag, then patiently wait, a twinkle of amusement in her eyes as she watched our hesitations in selecting the sweets we most preferred. It always seemed to be a stick or two of liquorice, a few aniseed balls, or sometimes a sherbet dip to share between the four of us on our homeward trek.

What idle capers we got up to on those return journeys. Our wild, youthful nature let loose in the rawness of the land, provoked adventures that often resulted in unexpected snippets of country ways coming to light. These wisps of knowledge we unconsciously stored, broadening the vast treasure of country lore we were acquiring.

Lowfold Cottages, Wisborough Green

It was just such an instance that occurred one day when we wandered off our usual path to a neighbouring farmer's land. The attraction was a rook colony we had noticed in a group of tall trees that stood isolated in the centre of a distant field. There were no dwellings that we could see, but we still kept close to the hedgerows to avoid being seen on private land. Then, with just a meadow to negotiate, we made an unobtrusive beeline over the open ground to the rookery. Scrambling through a barbed wire fence that circled the grove of trees, we slipped into the glade and there stood looking up at the high, swaying nests that showed dark against the blue of the sky.

The squabbling birds flew up in alarm at our noisy attempts to climb the great cumbersome elms. We shinned first up one, but could get no further than a few feet; then another, and another; but the sturdy trunks proved too much for our climbing skills. We lingered there some long while wondering how best to raid those inaccessible nests, our chatter rattling on but with no positive conclusion. Then, as if out of the blue, stepped the farmer – the incessant din of the squawking birds had drowned the sound of his approach through the wood, and we gawped in disbelief at being caught. He was a man of middle age, with greying hair and a stern, though not unfriendly face.

"What are you boys doing in here?" he roared.

"Only playing about mister," I mumbled, knowing full well that he knew we were after the rooks' eggs.

"Where are you from?" he continued in the same booming voice.

"Lowfold" we choroused.

"Well, you'd best get back there!" he demanded. "And don't let me catch you over here again, up at them nests."

A ripple of relief ran through me at being let off so lightly. We turned to go, then I hesitated, curiosity having pulled me up. I looked round to face the man.

"How'd you know we were here, mister?" I said.

"Well, just over there, on the far side of the field, lies my house," he said, pointing in the general direction indicated. "You won't have seen it, because it's in among them trees. But it's there. And with this rookery being so close, I knew straight away someone was about."

"Oh, right! We didn't know that, mister," I mumbled.

"No, you wouldn't," he replied. "You see, what you boys don't realise is that rooks don't build their nests very far from people. They likes company you see. Wherever there's a rookery, you're bound to find a house or two close by. So you won't make that mistake again, will you?"

"No, mister," I said, as we turned and scurried off home, a little wiser in the lore of the countryside.

14 The Dog's a Thief

While returning from one of our local shopping trips we found a young cuckoo, almost fledged, in a warbler's nest in the woodland. We brought the cute but bulky chap home to make a pet of him, but it was to no avail, for he did not survive the night in his makeshift cage. The following morning he was buried in a piece of waste ground at the far end of the garden with the due ceremony reserved for any of our pets that went the same way.

There was, though, one particular time when the burying of a favourite pet in this plot of land was discreetly ushered from our hands by Old Harry, with the best of intentions in mind. The animal concerned was our loveable old dog Judy, a black labrador. She had, a couple of months previously, given birth to seven or eight mongrel pups. One we kept, while the others had been found homes.

The day had opened warm and sunny, and the time was drawing on for midday. Being a Sunday, most of our neighbours were at home from work. Old Harry, his wife and a gathered group from the other cottages all stood in a circle chatting by our back door. They were too engrossed in their light hearted banter to take notice of Judy, who pattered about the vegetable patch, sniffing this and that, as dogs have a way of doing. The idle conversation continued with sporadic bursts of laughter that broke out occasionally in sharp cackles, the sound carrying through the woods in a series of echoes that softened the edges of the brassy notes.

A succulent smell of Sunday roast drifted from the various neighbours' open windows and doors in savoury wafts, eventually enticing the merry band to break up, each returning home. The old man wandered indoors, my mother in tow, her ever-busy nature forcing her to begin laying up our table for the midday meal. No sooner had she put the first couple of plates out than the old lady from the cottage next to ours appeared at our open door. She rattled the knocker furiously, then blurted out in a passion, "Nellie! I've just gone indoors and caught your dog eating the chicken I'd cooked and left on the table for our dinner!"

My mother looked up in horror.

"Oh no! Where's the dog now?" she cried in alarm.

"Don't know," fumed the distraught neighbour. "She ran off down the garden and into the woods I think."

Old Harry, who had overheard the woman, jumped up from the chair he had just occupied and stormed out of the door in search of the rogue dog. It was some long time before the animal was found and the whole unfortunate incident resolved in favour of the distressed woman.

The disgraced dog, having had a scolding from the old man for its bad ways, lay in its basket in the kitchen and was still looking sheepish when I came down stairs the following morning. Just before leaving for school I made my usual fuss of her and her pup, then I followed my brothers out of the door and down the lane. That afternoon when we returned the old dog was nowhere to be seen.

"Where's Judy, Mum?" I asked in a casual way.

"Gone," she replied.

"Gone! Gone where?" I said, persisting with my questions.

"Pop had to get rid of her," she muttered, as if to avoid the issue.

"What! Gave her away?" I continued.

"No. He had to put her down," she replied gravely. "He says that once a dog thieves, it'll always be a thief. So it was the only thing to do."

I stood there in the kitchen, numb with disbelief, while my mother went on to explain that as we could not afford a vet to have the old bitch put to sleep in an humane way, the old man had himself carried out the task. It seems he had taken her into the woods, tossed a rope over the bough of a tree and hanged her. Then he had buried the wretched animal on the spot where she had been killed.

The amusing antics of the two-month-old pup Rusty cushioned the blow of losing the old dog Judy to some extent. She was a loveable puppy that would always slip out of the door to chase us on our various errands. Lumbering up the path and out to the stony lane, we would encourage her to scamper after us, her clumsy games inciting fits of laughter as we raced ahead in high spirits. We took her on short playful runs to the end of the green lane or up as far as the farm, where, in the yard, she would skip and leap after the house martins as they swooped low in their hawking flights.

It was always fascinating to watch the swiftness of these birds as they skimmed the puddles in the cow yard, scooping beaks full of mud in their mission to build the nests in the beamed cart shed. Their sweet twitterings were often lost amid the incessant chirping that rang from the army of sparrows that resided under the eaves of the outbuildings. How delightful the sound of that tribe of birds; how homely it was to hear the flourished ring of their song! What was it about their excitable bickering that was always so reassuring? Perhaps it was that as long as there was livestock about the farm, there would always be corn scattered around the yard for these birds to eat – the lack of sparrows being a sure sign that a farm was long since dead and redundant.

Lowfold Farm in those far off days thrived with all kinds of farm stock. Chickens, ducks, guinea fowl and geese roamed the yard, and there were pigs and the pedigree herd of cows that Old Harry milked twice a day. The outlying fields also teemed with wildlife.

How well I remember during school holidays, working alone all day pulling docks in the cornfields, the inspiring song of the skylark cheering those laborious hours. It was always amusing to look up, squinting my eyes as I did so, and search the great expanse of blue for that heavenly songster. Often I would notice it rising towards the clouds, soaring so high that it became a speck in the deep ultramarine. Then it would vanish, yet its song still poured out in a clear, rich melody, thrilling the ears of the lone listener.

15 A Great Knot of Snakes

It was across the Lowfold fields that we would trek to a tributary of the River Arun to learn to swim, or just to paddle on hot summer days. On one drowsy morning we wandered in our careless way along that route. The sun was particularly hot, the day nodding by with only the soft humming of bees about the hedgerows.

Suddenly, at a place we had passed many times before, we unexpectedly walked into a great knot of grass snakes basking in the heat, on and around a table-sized tree stump. We stood there rooted to the spot, as we had never before seen such a massive number of these harmless reptiles accumulated in one place. Several that were sprawled about the grass slithered over to the writhing lump on the sawn tree as we approached. We gingerly made our way through the ugly mass, spotting as we did so a smaller batch that lay strung about the sun-drenched side of a corn rick close by. We carried on down to the river, still feeling uneasy at having seen such an extraordinary large tangle of snakes, of which we thought there must have been as many as seventy or eighty together.

Within a short time our high spirits and hoots of youthful laughter, always so apparent when we played and bathed in those cool luxuriant waters, washed away all thoughts of that great bundle of reptiles. On returning across the fields and along the stony lane to home, we gave them no more thought.

There were times when we played so long over by the river that it was almost dark when we made our way back up the lane to home. It was then, on those warm late summer evenings, just when dusk was falling, that the old flint lane took on a more serene stillness, an inexplicable hush. Here and there, along the grass verges, the tiny fluorescent lanterns of the glow-worms would light up, as if to guide us on our return to the cottage.

In stark contrast, there were days in the wet winter season, when the deep ruts along this route turned to flooding streams which gushed down a natural fall in the surface and emptied into the woods.

It was down this stony slope that I came a cropper one day while astride and free-wheeling a rickety old bike we had found. I was nearly knocked cold as I crashed head on with the flints in the lane. The rusting bike fared the worse, for it fell apart on impact. The buckled frame, along with one of the wheels. was slung back on the dump from where it had come, while the other wheel had a further use. Out of devilment, I shinned up an oak tree close to the entrance of the stony road and threaded a spindly branch through the spokes. There it hung, twenty feet high, a suspended trophy, a reminder of my wild, youthful days.

A few weeks after the push-bike crash the old man took it into his head to move yet again, to another farm job. What his reason for leaving Lowfold was, I never enquired. It was, though, as I recall, not too far off my thirteenth birthday, when the day finally arrived to wave goodbye to our friends in that tiny row of cottages. Our new place of residence was to be the great farmhouse of Freehold Farm, Northchapel.

16 The Return to Lowfold

Almost fifty years passed before I had the opportunity to wander again over the Lowfold farmland that I knew so well as a child. The outlying fields looked the same – welcoming, old fashioned and wonderfully picturesque, with the River Arun winding a sleepy course through the buttercup meadows. The once familiar scent of camomile still wafted its fragrant perfume, to greet me again as I wandered the footpaths. It heartened me to catch its sweet smell and to see it still growing in abundant strips and patches along my old haunts. There too, I noticed the old wind-pump: the well acquainted landmark of those distant days still lay across the field.

One or two skylarks soared up and hovered in the heavens as I ambled back to the farm, inspiring an even greater pleasure to my walk. The old farm buildings, though, appeared a sorry sight, disused and neglected to some degree. Wandering over to the cart shed, I peered in, but could see no sign of the house martins' nests. There was too, an uncomfortable quietness about the yard. It took me a little time to realise it was the lack of those squabbling, chirping sparrows that was the cause. As I turned to go, the old farmer, Steve Osmaston, suddenly appeared at the door of an outbuilding. Always the true gentleman he greeted me in a friendly way.

"Hi!" I said, smiling broadly. "My old step dad, Harry Pateman, worked here years ago. Not sure whether you remember him? Anyway, I thought it would be interesting to look round the place again."

The old gentleman's face beamed with pleasure as he recalled Harry and his family. We talked of old times and new.

"The farm is not as it used to be," he said gravely. Then he went on to explain, with eyes watering, that after years of building up his pedigree herd of dairy cows he had been forced to sell them due to the recent decline in farming. We talked some more, until it was time for me to go.

"You know you can walk round my farm at any time!" he said, as I ambled out the yard. "Walk anywhere you like. And if anyone says anything, tell them I said you could."

I looked over my shoulder and thanked him heartily, then turned on to the lane and walked down past our once-loved cottage.

The old dwelling appeared unaltered, while the rutted lane, I noticed, had long since been laid with tarmac. The ugly, grey surface seemed to me out of character in such a pretty country setting.

Soon I reached the end of the smooth road, and as I did so, something made me look up. There, suspended high, still hung my childhood trophy, the rusting bike wheel. The spokes had fallen away, but the rim remained, grown in and all part of the sturdy bough that held it there.

I smiled with an inner joy. For I was once again a wild, carefree child, climbing that tree with boyish daring.

17 The Homely Old Farmhouse

The rambling old farmhouse of Freehold Farm lay over a mile up a dead-end lane. Branching off the main Petworth to Northchapel road, the route to the homestead weaved through ancient woodland, first passing Pheasant Court Farm, then on and out to the more open scenery of grass fields and cropped hedges. Nearing the last quarter of the journey, the track dropped steeply to the recess of a hollow, which was flanked by dense copseland. Here it levelled sufficiently to span a tiny, babbling brook, then soon began its breathless climb to again reach open fields. It was at this point that across the great stretch of grassland, Freehold Farm, with its cluster of barns, first came into view.

Freehold Farm with its cluster of old barns, 1957

How well I remember, during the short days of winter, those daunting travels along this lonely lane when returning home each day from school – walking alone, with hurried steps, through the darkening tunnels of overhanging trees; the spine-chilling shivers that ran down my back when approaching feet disturbed roosting birds, their rustling in the blackest shadows spurring a brisker pace towards the last leg of the journey; and that sigh of relief when at last I glimpsed the distant light that seemed to twinkle in the window of the far-away farmhouse. Then the final dash across frosty fields, my constant short-cut home on those cold winter nights. On reaching the garden I would fly in through the gate, skate up the icy path, then come abruptly to a halt by the back door. Having regained my breath, I would open it and, in a matter of fact way, wander in, as if to make out I was no more concerned about the long, moonlight walk home than the bats that flitted about the eaves of the old house.

The back door opened into the scullery, a cool, spacious room devoid of furniture other than an old solid wooden chair and a green-painted Victorian mangle. The floor was made up of red bricks, scuffed shallow in places by the endless comings and goings of heavy boots. There was, too, a deep masonry sink and a massive copper boiler clad in old stonework that my mother used twice a week. A log fire kept alight in the bowels of this tub always ensured that our clothes were boiled clean, the whites bleached white.

At the far corner of the room there were two doors, the first, to the left, leading down to the cold, black depths of an enormous cellar (a place to which we rarely ventured), the other leading into the hall and stairwell, where, at the foot of the great open stairs, was the entrance to the kitchen, the hub of the house. Here, my mother performed miracles with her meagre weekly shopping allowance. Joints of meat were cooked to perfection, pork scratchings sizzled, jam tarts, apple dumplings and everyone's favourite, bacon pudding, steamed and baked to a delectable taste on the hot plates of the great Aga. The succulent smells that wafted from this busy chamber and drifted out to the garden to greet healthy appetites were legendary.

Beyond a well scrubbed oak table that was used as a work top, a short passage on the far side of the kitchen passed by the redundant front door. This heavily bolted main entrance was always hidden by a substantial, bottle green curtain. The cupboard-sized corridor was the entrance to the sitting room, which looked out to the most picturesque views of old meadows, strewn with daisies and patches of bright yellow buttercups. Often, in these fields, we would gather hoards of fresh mushrooms during autumn seasons. The landscape further away was edged by the venerable oaks of Wet Wood. Then, as a backdrop, the grey curves of Blackdown Hill rose, mountainous, to complete the scene.

My mother's eccentric passion for collecting unusual items, picked up for a few shillings at jumble and farm sales, had grown so much that the house by then displayed objects of fascination in every nook and cranny. The front room was laden with perhaps the most curious. There was an antelope's head, with a fine pair of curved antlers, all stuffed and set upon a smartly varnished shield. This animal's bust, with its vacantly staring glass eyes, hung as a feature on the wall to the right of the north-facing window. The wall opposite displayed another deer's head, below which was suspended a stuffed pygmy alligator. The spaces between these freakish objects were filled by various 'Miss Pears' prints and a fine picture of the dog 'Prince', the First World War mascot. There were also several old family photos that took pride of place beside the mantle clock which stood on a shelf above the fire.

Not content with this striking display of ornaments, the old lady had crammed more of her peculiar exhibits along the surface of the sideboard. There stood a beautiful stuffed green woodpecker,

The stuffed pygmy alligator

Jim and Bill Pateman and David Johnston

protected from dust by a perfectly domed glass cover. Beside this decorative bird was arranged a number of ammonites. But the most amazing specimen of all was the dried skull, with serrated bill, of a swordfish. For strangers entering the room for the first time it was a place that inspired immediate interest, arresting the attention and drawing the eyes from one curious artefact to another.

With the door closed to keep out the cold draughts of a winter evening, the sitting room took on a special old-fashioned charm and an indescribable cosiness of its own. The great down-hearth fire, stoked with huge logs, would roar all evening, with shadows from the flames dancing and leaping about the ceiling and walls. They would sporadically light up the pictures, or briefly reflect onto the glass dome of the woodpecker, with, too, a glint of light falling momentarily on the staring eyes of the stuffed deer heads. The pendulum of the mantle clock would swing with a homely tick, tock, tick, tock, the movement having a peaceful, comforting effect, the old brass oil lamp casting its dim light over the wine-coloured table cloth and the old man puffing contentedly on his pipe while staring vacantly into the flames of the fire. His clothes reeked incessantly of farmyard smells, the odour sometimes so strong that it wafted out to the kitchen and filtered to the upper rooms, contaminating the whole house. There he would sit, very nearly motionless, the billows of smoke sucked from his pipe drifting like a blue mist about his chair. And so the evening would pass.

There was, though, one particular time when the lighting of the front room fire disturbed the treasured peace of the house. The kindling sticks were no doubt more damp than usual on that day, so it took measures beyond the favoured method of lighting crumpled paper beneath the wood to get it to burn. Placing the centre broad sheet of the local Gazette over the gaping mouth of the hearth, my brother Tony held it there, allowing the fast flowing air to draw the flames. It was always a risky business, for the up-draught in the great chimney was so powerful that, as we often joked, "It would almost suck your boots off, if you were too close to the fire."

As it was, the wood soon caught alight and roared up the flue. Then suddenly, without warning, the outstretched paper was snatched from his hands and pulled high up the chimney, catching alight as it did so. Both he and I tried to retrieve it, but it was no use: it had been sucked up and out of sight.

As luck would have it, Old Harry arrived home from work about the same time the freak accident occurred. He strode into the room and noticed immediately – something was wrong.

"What's happened?" he said striding towards us.

"The paper's gone up the chimney, Pop!" replied Tony, with a sheepish look on his face.

The old man knelt beside the fire, swivelled his head round and peered up the cavernous flue.

"Can't see anything alight up there boy!" he said. "I'll have a look outside, see if there are any sparks coming out the chimney."

He wandered out into the chill night air still mumbling, then returned after a few minutes declaring that all seemed safe.

We settled down for the evening, stoking the fire with a few hefty logs. Half an hour later and the old man thought he should check that all was well. He made a brief excursion to the garden, and then returned in seconds, rushing back through the door in alarm.

"The chimney's alight!" he shouted. "Sparks flying out the top of it!"

He bolted up the stairs to the bedroom where the chimney breast passed up through to the roof. We hurried on behind. Coming to a halt in the room he spread both hands over the plaster to test the heat.

"Douse that fire downstairs, Mother!" he bellowed. "The bricks are red hot up here! I'll have to go to the farm and get the guvner to phone the fire brigade."

He shot off down the stairs and out of the door in his panic-stricken pursuit to get help from Pheasant Court Farm. His greatest fear was that, due to having no phone, and along with the very remoteness in which the house was situated, there was every chance the fire might well spread and gut the house before the fire brigade arrived. As it was, when they did turn up over an hour later, the tremendous heat generated in the chimney had made the breast wall in the bedroom so hot that it was impossible to lay a hand on the plaster work.

With the arrival of the fire engine the disaster was soon under control. We then sat well into the night, counting our blessings at the happy conclusion. During that excited chatter Old Harry boasted that, as he had no bicycle or other means of transport, he had run, regardless of his age, full speed the three-quarters of a mile to the farm for help. The sheer terror and worry of that evening, whatever the man's actions, had certainly drained all energy and taken its toll on him and his wife, for when we made our way upstairs to bed their tired old faces looked drawn and white.

"G'night, Mum! 'Night, Pop!" we all said in tired, drifting voices.

" 'Night, you boys!" was their distant reply.

The impressive oak staircase led straight up to a balcony, with simple carved railings as a safety fixture. The complete structure overlooked the hall from directly above the rising stairs. Four bedrooms led off from this open-sided corridor, three to the right facing east, and one at the far end facing west. The latter was always my parents' bedroom.

The first room at the top of the stairs looked out over a cluster of old farm buildings, grouped together to form an enclosed yard for livestock. A massive, 17th-century oak barn was the main feature, flanked at both ends by cattle hovels of a similar period. The great age of these structures had mellowed to such a rustic charm that they appeared to have sprouted out of the ground and were all part of the natural landscape.

Of the three rooms I periodically slept in during those years we lived in the house, this was perhaps the most pleasant. It was always comforting to open sleepy eyes of a morning in this light and airy chamber and hear the gentle stirrings of cattle down in the yard, or the farmer and his stockman rising before dawn to tend the hungry beasts with hay and straw while deprived of the fresh open fields. I would catch the sound of the men's earthy voices drifting up to the window in muted phrases, their harmonious babble

*Our dog Rusty in the garden of Freehold
Farmhouse, 1958. Note
the antiquated cultivator behind him*

occasionally broken by Old Harry's infectious laughter, followed by softer mutterings as they again resumed their essential labours – a smile forming on the lips of the musing listener, as the mind was set to wondering what harmless prank the old man had played to spark the full-bodied jocular outburst.

Such treasured memories separate this peaceful room from the others. The middle bedroom was a dark, oak-beamed sanctuary that escaped my attention, for I only used the space as a temporary measure for a couple of weeks. The third and final refuge I occupied over the greatest period of time. With the window facing north, it was always the coldest chamber. How I shivered during the bitter nights of winter, with only a blanket or two, and a few heavy overcoats as a cover on the old iron bed! I would rise bitterly cold, then stagger to the window to scrape ice from the inside of the pane, if only to peer with bleary eyes at the sheets of white frost that covered the fields.

The warmest room was the old man's and his wife's, the west-facing bedroom. It was through this sunny space that we would

Freehold Farmhouse – stepbrother Billy working in the garden

traipse on our trips to the attic. A tiny door in the far corner of their room was the entrance to a cramped set of stairs that corkscrewed up to the two light and airy lofts. At the top-most step a door opened into the east facing apartment, always known as 'the museum room'. All the knick-knacks, artefacts and objects of obscure use or existence cluttered up the tables in this little haven. Birds' nests, birds' eggs, odd and fanciful pieces of wood with interesting peeling bark, shepherds' crowns, minute flint arrow-heads and all description of dried and pressed flowers and umpteen scrapbooks, all lay piled, one upon another, as evidence of my mother's obsession to collect and hoard.

The attic room opposite, facing west, I somehow managed to claim as my art studio. Here, I finally graduated from simple pencil sketches to my very first attempts at painting with water colours. Poor examples as they were, I found amusement and a quiet pride in the amateur representations of the countryside I produced. The old man, though, found no interest or value in the time that I spent creating such whimsical art work.

"That'll never get you anywhere!" he would grumble. "You wanna git off out there, and do some proper work. Doing that ain't gonna earn ya livin'! Come on, git off out there to the shed, an' saw some wood for your mother."

To protest was useless, so I always silently obeyed. But there were of course, those opportune times when I was able to sneak up to this convenient loft to enjoy my pastime of sketching and painting.

The window to my tiny studio looked out from below the half-hipped gable of the house and down to the sizeable garden. Further afield, the views stretched over acres of undulating meadows and ancient woodlands. There was, too, the advantage from this high point of catching the first glimpse of Old Harry as he returned from work. Far away, his figure could be seen trudging home along the long and weary lane. Then it was time to pack up the paints and race off out to the shed, saw in hand, as a proof of my willing industry.

18 The Foxhunt Runs Riot

One day, while working in the old beamed outhouse, my ears pricked up at the distinct note of the hunting horn pealing in the distance. The sound soon drew close, with the baying of the hounds as accompaniment to the rousing notes that blasted from the instrument. Dropping the bow-saw that I was using, I leapt out of the shed just in time to catch a glimpse of the fox racing through our garden.

The hounds, in full cry, were close on its tail bursting through every crevice, gap and convenient space in the hedge. Then came the huntsmen, scarlet coats astride massive, sweating beasts, fully airborne as they cleared the well trimmed hawthorn barrier. Bringing up the rear were the less experienced riders, the velveteen, jet-clad followers who bulldozed a path through the quick-set jump in their determined, clumsy pursuit.

I stood rooted to the spot in total amazement. Their audacious contempt at running amok over ground occupied by a humble farm labourer appeared to me almost comical. Caught up in the tunnel of excitement, they tore on through our plot like a whirlwind and disappeared through the far hedge as fast as they had arrived.

It was about then that the old man appeared at the door to see what the commotion was. He stood there for some minutes with a face like thunder, then strutted over and surveyed in silence the destruction to his beloved vegetable garden, the ploughed-up borders and the sorry state of the quick-set hedge. Then he vowed to "have things put right!"

There was no forgiveness in the man, despite his usual enthusiasm for the hunt. He stormed down the lane to the farm, to have words with his governor.

"How dare they," he said, "ride through here like a posse of vandals! Just as if it's their God-given right to trample over people's seeds and plants!"

He soon had his way, for in no time at all his veg and flower beds were hastily put in order. All was then forgotten.

Apart from this one particular sorry event, the fox hunt was, to all of us, always a joy to see and hear. The first sound of the horn, its familiar notes blowing in the far-away meadows, would be our signal to rush with great excitement to catch a glimpse of them. There we would stand in the expectation that they might come our way, if only to open field gates to let them through. For on those fortunate occasions a silver half-crown was always passed into our hand by the last gentleman rider to go through. We would then pursue them on foot, running for all our worth to keep up with the hunters and the hounds.

19 A Long-Lost Mill

Within the great stretch of woodland known as Wet Wood stood an isolated cottage, once the residence of an old game-keeper. The dwelling when we first discovered it was in a state of serious decay. It was during our first school holiday at Freehold that we romped through this great wood in search of amusement. Un-expectedly we came to the relic of an old wicket gate hanging at an angle on its one rusting hinge. The sizeable garden before us had been taken over by a tangle of briars and nettles. This dense growth, we were unaware, concealed a treacherously deep well. A jungle of climbers crept up the grey stone walls of the old place and prised a route under the eaves, dislodging ceiling lathes, rafters and slates to find light again above the warped line of ridge tiles.

We forced our way through the thick-set brambles, razor sharp thorns savagely cutting our legs as we edged forward to the suspiciously open front door. Tony peered warily in, as if he half expected to be greeted by some resident ghoul.

"What's in there, Tone?" I whispered.

His answer was interrupted by Billy, who had gripped my arm while craning his neck from behind.

"Looks spooky in there, don't it?" he whispered nervously.

"It's all right," replied Tony, easing the creaking door an inch or two and walking in. We all followed one behind the other and there, just inside the entrance, we paused, straining our eyes in the gloom. It did not take long to become accustomed to the bad light. We could soon make out scattered shards of plaster that lay about the floor, broken glass, great clumps of rotting wallpaper and an old pair of moth-eaten curtains still hanging in their place at the window. The rank smell of decay lingered strong and foul in the confined room. We crept gingerly through to the stairwell, where the rising steps hung precariously in space: the floorboards in an adjoining chamber had given way, dislodging the complete structure.

Here we climbed, each hoisting the other to the safety of the one remaining bedroom that in appearance was fairly sound, with its sturdy oak floor still in place. Although damp, and reeking of mildew, the room was in remarkably good condition compared with the remainder of the house. We loitered there a while.

It was then, in the stillness of the moment, that we became aware of a peculiar soft, fluting noise faintly audible above our heads. We strained our ears.

"What is it?" whispered Jim, with a puzzled look.

"Don't know! Maybe it's a ghost, " I replied, a little amused by the thought.

We listened a little longer, and then Tony put in his views.

"Think it's pigeons!" he said. "But I don't know how they would have got in there!"

We wandered out to the rotting stairs where, above, we noticed a closed trap-door in the ceiling.

"Here, Dave, stand on my shoulders and open it, if you can," said my eldest brother, clasping his hands together as a foothold to aid my climb.

The square loft hatch was easily raised and I peered into the dusky space. There, by the far end gable, the sunlight poured in through a gaping hole in the roof, the shaft of light illuminating a great flock of fantail doves.

"Doves!" I yelled. "Pure white doves. Hundreds of 'em."

My brothers clambered up beside me to see the great flock of birds for themselves.

"Cor! Ain't they lovely! I'm gonna see if I can catch one and take 'im home for a pet," shouted Jim, lumbering clumsily forward with arms outstretched.

"Mind how you go!" warned Tone, who kept close on his heels.

But it was too late. The reckless lad dived, grabbing a bird with that first swoop. There was a crash, followed by a great billow of dust that flew up as he disappeared through the rotten beams. At the same instant the flock of birds rose in alarm at the sudden disturbance. Feathers, cobwebs and choking clouds of grime swirled round in the confined space, as the doves flapped in panic to find freedom through the hole in the roof.

Tony held fast his young brother's feet, as the lad struggled to climb back up and into the loft. But it was no use, he was stuck fast. His head and shoulders poked down through the ceiling into the bedroom below, while his legs, painfully speared with the needle sharp splinters of broken lathes, were anchored in place.

"I've got your feet, Jim," shouted Tony. "So you can't fall. Dave'll help you get down into the bedroom. He'll be there in a minute."

I leapt down through the loft hatch, then into the bedroom below. There hung Jim, his arms flaying in the breeze, his sooty face a picture of terror. He was soon lowered to the floor, with legs bruised and grazed, his clothes smudged with grime. He stood beside me looking sheepish, his pride having taken a beating.

"Pity," I said with a devilish grin. "I was hoping we was gonna get one as a pet. Suppose we could climb up there and try again when they've settled down."

"No! I damn well ain't!" he sniffled. "I ain't gettin' up there again."

As we came away from the old ruin we fell about laughing at how he had suddenly disappeared through the ceiling, legs kicking in the air, a hundred white doves taking off around him in one great swoop. We ribbed him until he flared up in anger, and then our boisterous moods ceased, replaced by quieter chat, directed on ideas of how those pink-eyed birds came there. We guessed they must have been left at the house by the last occupant, then multiplied over the years, roosting in the loft when a hole appeared in the decaying roof.

As we wandered on through the great forest, the path we trekked led to a sizeable fir plantation. Here we discovered a number of giant wood-ant nests, each constructed of millions of pine needles, all meticulously worked to form a metre-high dome. We watched in fascination the comings and goings of those busy ants, which must have numbered many hundreds of thousands. We poked their domain with our hazel sticks, testing the resilience of the workers that strove to repair the damage. Then, soon tired of our wanton destruction, we ambled on up the path.

The landscape suddenly opened out to a large expanse of marshy ground in the form of a deep basin. Through this sunken hollow a tiny stream had cut a course and then passed on through an old mill-race, before disappearing beneath the path where we stood. We leapt down to the stone wall of this ancient water course and there lingered, for it was one of those places that captivated the imagination, a place that inspired teenage minds with thoughts of adventure. For us it was a spot to which we were to return time and again during the period we lived at Freehold.

The site of this favourite haunt proved to be the remains of the long-lost Chaffold Mill. The dam, measuring about 85 metres in length, was constructed by one John Kitchener in 1370. The mill, built at the north end of this dam, had long since gone, and all that remained was the wheel-pit, water-race and waste bypass. Two massive elliptical arches, typical of 14th-century construction, spanned the water-race and served as a bridge along which carts would have travelled on the breast of the pond bay. It seems that the lake drained naturally when the mill became ruinous in the mid - 17th century, leaving in its place the hollow basin of wasteland.

The stream, caught in the narrow channel of the mill-race, surged with greater force through the massive arched subway, emerging to the east of the bridge in a wonderful cascading waterfall. A cool, dark lagoon had been formed by this ever-gushing cataract, the plunge resulting in a constant circle of mini whirlpools that rippled out to obscurity in the shaded pool. Here, in this clear luxuriant water, we would trawl our butterfly nets in search of minnows, scooping handfuls of tiny pebbles, rotting sediment and occasionally a freshwater shrimp in the process. Often we would clamber up the vertical walls of the bridge, testing our climbing skills in the footholds of the great masonry construction. Beneath the arches of this bridge we discovered the nest of a grey wagtail. The erratic antics of this bird, its incessant flitting from stone to stone and its short restless flights, were always amusing to observe.

But that which held the greatest wonder was the awesome light which penetrated this glade at certain times of the year. For on that side where tumbled the water, the overhanging trees kept the combe in constant shade throughout the mid-summer days. Come evening, the scarlet sun, low in the sky, fell in line with the arched subway. It was then that a radiant shaft of sunlight beamed through the passage, as if by the guidance of some magical hand. The rippled water and broad-leafed trees within the tiny glen would then be cast in deep crimson tones, the whole scene a mystical charm, a curious beauty.

20 A Boat Trip Turns Sour

The lake known as Shillinglee, a couple of miles distant as the crow flies from Freehold, was a place to which we occasionally trekked.

On one particular summer morning we made our way over to this great expanse of water. Wandering past the old Mill Farm that lay at the head of the reservoir we ambled on and round to the side directly opposite to that which we had come. It was a warm, sunny day, and in carefree mood we searched the reeded banks for wildfowl nests. The farm slipped further away as we slowly progressed along our route.

Unexpectedly we came to a small dinghy moored up in the seclusion of a dense growth of rushes. Young Jim, walking ahead of us, was first to see it.

"Hey! Look at this," he yelled. "C'mon, lets have a go in it!"

Wading excitedly into the shallow water he leapt aboard.

"C'mon!" he again urged, his high spirits having got the better of him. "Look! There's even a rowing oar."

We all climbed into the tiny vessel, the keen sailor handing me the paddle he had discovered stored in the bilges. The mooring rope was released and we set off across the water, the little boat zig-zagging on its unsteady course by way of the irregular sweep of the single oar. We swiftly reached the centre of the lake.

Our amusement, though, was not to last, for we soon caught the distant sound of a man bellowing from the direction of the farm. Stretching our eyes to the shoreline we could just make out the stout figure of the farmer whose boat we dared to row without permission. We had seen him a number of times before, pottering about the outbuildings, feeding his livestock or generally making himself busy. But we had never spoken to him, and he had never found cause to have words with any of us – although he certainly did have reason now.

Waving his arms frantically, he bawled out in a fair rage that we were "to return the dingy immediately". There was no option. We turned the boat to face the music, and paddled back in the direction from which we had come. Seeing the course we were taking, the old farmer broke into a trot, coming at a good pace towards the moorings. My heart raced as we drew near, for the furious man had closed the gap to no more than a dozen or so yards. I could hear his agonising gasps for breath; see his purple, puffed face contorted as he raced the last few feet.

"Blow this!" I muttered, drawing hard on the oar to turn the craft away from land, catching the whites of the wild man's eyes as I did so.

Frantically, I set the boat for the opposite shore, while he, the mad farmer, seeing the sudden turn of events, cursed aloud our devious ways as he leapt up and down on the muddy bank. But I cared not, for my one aim was to escape his wrath by reaching the fields that lay on the far side of the lake. The fuming man then turned and sped away, in a vain attempt to beat us there.

"Get paddling with your hands!" I yelled to my brothers. "Or he'll get there before us!"

It had all, suddenly, become a desperate race. The faster he ran, the faster we paddled, breaking, I am sure, the speed record for any one-oared rowing race – for it took no time at all to reach the safety of those distant meadows. Scrambling out of the little boat we raced away, leaving the vessel to float wherever the breeze took it.

Glancing back, I just caught the figure of the frantic man, still running for all his worth the full perimeter of the shore-line. He was less than half way round, so I knew he had no chance of catching us. But we bolted over the fields all the same, reaching the safety of home without ever being caught for our mischief.

21 Woodland Rides on a Motorbike

About halfway down the lane from Freehold to Pheasant Court Farm, a track leads off to the left, through a narrow neck of woodland. Each morning I would meet a school friend, who made her way along this well-worn woodland path to join me on my daily trek to school. She lived in a tiny red-brick cottage at the far end of the spinney with her mother, Mrs. Carver, a woman in her late fifties.

The only form of transport owned by this middle-aged lady was a rather archaic motorcycle and side-car. When driving this aged machine she always dressed in an old 'bomber' flying jacket and brown leather skullcap, with glass goggles of the First World War period. Perched on the ageing 'Ariel' combination, in the image of a veteran flying ace, she would charge through the woods, the side-car careering on the rough track as she weaved her way through the trees. On reaching the open lane the throbbing engine would burst into a vibrant roar and she would take off in a flurry of dust and smoke along the less rugged route.

On those occasions when I called at the house for her daughter, Bridget, I would be asked in and directed to a seat by the old iron range. Here the tiny kitchen was ever warm, always the very essence of homely cottage life. The dwelling, like our own house, had no electricity or modern conveniences, yet it was always cosy, despite its basic essentials. The rear windows looked out on an adequately-sized vegetable plot, where the soil was rich and black from years of constant turning. The flower garden facing the house, half the size to that in the rear, had a path of ancient stone slabs placed down the centre in single file, leading out to the woodland ride.

This access route led off to a most enchanting walk in the summer months. The track falls gently away until you come to a tiny pack-horse bridge, the single arch spanning an ever flowing river. Here, the currents softly dance as they buff the sedge green banks, while perpetual ringlets are formed by slender reeds as the water glides on its meandering course. The path further on gradually rises parallel with a steep and natural formation of sandstone that flanks the route, forming a sunken lane of enduring charm. Beneath the broad-leafed trees that form a canopy of constant shade, clusters of hart's-tongue fern thrive. Within a quarter of a mile, this cool and rugged cloister opens out to the sun and continues on to Colehook, a tiny hamlet close to the little village of Ebernoe.

What fun we had in this remote woodland village on fair day. Always held on the 25th July, the Ebernoe Horn Fair was an event not to be missed by the country people far and wide, and we were no exception. We would fall in with the usual frolics organised by the locals. Cheering on the cricket team, at the start of the morning match, was something enjoyed by all ages. Clapping hands would sporadically erupt, with echoes that rattled through the quiet forest like the clatter of so many machine guns firing in salute. As time drew on we would wander off to the far side of the playing field to watch with hungry eyes the basting of the horned sheep. The massive carcass was turned over and over on a great roasting spit which spanned an open fire placed in the corner of the fairground. The old fashioned merry-go-rounds and numerous other attractions would soon take our pennies, and so the day would merrily pass. We would then amble off home in the consuming dusk of evening. The rousing humdrum of the fair would dwindle to a faint drone as we travelled through the woods, then on and out to the more open farmland. Here, in the centre of a meadow, stood the quaintly picturesque cottage called Bittlesham.

This isolated dwelling had no access lane or road leading to it, other than the footpath that passed by the front door on its winding course through the field. It was, as I recall, a beautiful old house with half-hipped gables and a long tiled roof that sagged wearily along the ridge, owing to its great age. The roof to the rear sloped down to within two feet of the ground, with a couple of windows looking out on to the back garden at almost ground level. It had been, I believe, in times gone by, part of an old farm, with barns and animal hovels that must have made a pretty picture. The outbuildings had long since gone when I knew it, but there still lingered an old-fashioned charm about the place.

It was in this house that old George Goatcher once lived. He, for reasons that I never came to know, moved out of the homely cottage and came to lodge with us at Freehold. He was an elderly man, born in the early years of the 1880s. His stature was tall and lean, though his age had wearied his hoary figure to a stoop, creating a hump that merged into round shoulders. The only other peculiarity he displayed was a grossly deformed thumb and forefinger on the right hand, a consequence, he once told me, of being struck by lightning while out chopping logs for the fire. The bolt of lightning, it seems, had struck the anvil he was using, hurling it several feet away, the shock throwing him off his feet. His hand, so severely burnt, never healed to its former condition.

Of an evening, this venerable countryman could often be persuaded to play a few tunes on his mouth organ, for which he had a natural talent. The instrument would be fetched from his room and a few notes played to "warm up". Soon feet would begin to fidget as the rhythm gained in pace, and the evening would pass in a variety of old country tunes.

Old George only stayed with us for about six to eight months, but during that time I came to know him as a quiet, soft-spoken and inoffensive man. He was, for sure, the original 'gentle giant'.

I well recall one day when I stood outside our back door, occupied with the tedious task of fixing the wheels back on a battered Dinky toy for Billy. I had not been there long before the hoary figure of George wandered in through the garden gate and up the path towards me.

"Hi ya, Mister Goatcher!" I said as I looked up to greet him. "I seem to have got myself an impossible job here. Think it's broken for good."

I held up the irreparable toy to show him. He took it, examined it, then with a broad smile passed it back.

"We used to make our own toys when we were children," he chuckled.

"Oh! How'd you make the wheels then?" I asked.

"Ah, you had to have patience for that job," he replied. "You see, we would get a piece of black slate and a large staple. Hold one point of the staple on to the slate as a boring tool for the centre. Then turn the staple round and round in the same place, and the other point would then scrape out the circle for a wheel."

The idea seemed well worth trying, so I soon knocked up a small model car with the aid of hammer, nails and a few odd scraps of wood. The black slate took a little longer to acquire – a couple of weeks, in fact. The little toy was then complete, with perfectly round slate wheels, all running with ease on tiny tin-tack axles.

And Billy? Well yes, he was 'chuffed to boots' with his unexpected present.

22 A Farm Auction

The necessity of 'shift and make do' had taught us all the art, or skill, of construction. How often had we thrown together a few planks of timber to make a rabbit hutch, or hurriedly made a new and sturdy sawing horse for the cutting up of cordwood into logs. These were jobs we had done time and again, and we thought nothing of making such things.

With this in mind, there can be no surprise at our amazement when Old Harry decided to buy a 'ready-made' chicken coop, all inclusive of nesting boxes and wire run – a construction we could easily have knocked up, had he asked. He and my mother had been to a local farm auction, close to Northchapel, and had purchased the entire coop. Then he had got his governor to run the thing home on the tractor and trailer. Perhaps he had got caught up in the bidding fever.

There is no doubt that farm auctions are fascinating events. They draw the crowds from miles around and encourage the punters to bid, by way of the very rare antiquity of the goods and chattels being sold. For there is none so great a hoarder of old things than a farmer.

The outbuildings and farmyard are often sources of unending interest, full of rusting tools and long since redundant machinery. There the implements lie, grown into masses of nettles and tangles of thorns, all discarded and, in appearance, unwanted.

Old Harry, that shrewd old countryman, once told me, "You can ask a farmer if he will sell you anything that you may have seen lying unused about his farm. The reply will always be the same, a refusal.

"The farmer," he would say, "seems to have the attitude of 'I don't want it, but you ain't having it.' "

That was the old man's views on the hoarding habits of our farmers.

Come the time to eventually sell up, an auction would be arranged and all the farm implements, some pieces going back hundreds of years, would be pulled out as exhibits to go under the hammer.

This, in a small way, is how the old man and my mother accumulated so many of their antiquated items over the years. And there, in the garden of Freehold, we would often find ourselves busy using some tool from a bygone age to cultivate the hard clay soil, at Old Harry's behest.

23 Guy Fawkes Night

How peaceful our garden, that well cultivated piece of ground! There, while working on warm summer days, I would often notice an unaccountable stillness, a pause in the soft breathing of the land. Far away sounds would then be heightened, become more noticeable. The hoots of the children playing on the village green in Northchapel, two miles away, would drift over the great woodland and across the meadows. Softened by the distance, their voices would rise, and then taper off in diluted strains – miniature threads that would float on a breath of warm air to the listener in the remote garden. The drone of a bee in the flower bed would distract the ear; the movement of a butterfly skitting about the vegetable plot might catch the eye; and that magical, silent pause would be lost. Then it was back to my task of plucking the ever choking weeds from the rows of plants, a task we were all happy to do on those memorable summer days.

There were times when I would look up and notice a few deer that had wandered out from the cool woods afar, to graze in the simmering hay fields, or watch with amusement the skulking habits of pheasants as they crept about the meadows, their seemingly pointless wanderings being never too far from the cover of hedgerows. It was for me, in those teenage years, more of a joy than a chore to work in this isolated garden, to fully absorb the passing of the seasons and to take in the differing shades of the ever changing landscape.

How well I recall those cold, crisp autumn days, the icy sun lying low in the sky of a late afternoon, the outlying meadows a wondrous sea of gossamers. Hundreds of millions of those silky webs lay like a bed of lace spread across the grass fields, the cold, cold sun highlighting the strange phenomenon with a breathtaking silver tint.

With the drawing in of winter there was always the trimming of garden hedges and the cutting of those odd clumps of shrubbery. The lopped branches of thorns and brambles we invariably heaped up in a corner of the vegetable plot as a reserve for bonfire night. Come the 5th November, the great mound of briars was always well dried and burned wonderfully.

The very last Guy Fawkes night that I spent at Freehold proved to be an event I would never forget, for my mother had brought a cheap box of fireworks that strangely came with the old man's blessing. The assortment, made up of a few bangers, sparklers, rockets, Roman candles and Catherine wheels, was shared equally among my brothers. My selection I deposited in my coat pocket.

The bonfire that evening, fanned by the chill night air, flared high, lighting the wild, lonely countryside like a mysterious beacon. I wandered innocently from the family group, walked round the burning mass and there lingered in the shadows. Then, glancing through the haze of smoke, I eyed the old man, who was occupied with the setting up of a Roman candle, opposite me. Feeling safe, I pulled a crumpled Woodbine from my pocket and put a match to it warily, as a schoolboy smoker will. I drew heavily on the cigarette, keeping an eye on Old Harry as I did so, for he knew nothing of my smoking experiments.

Suddenly he turned and walked past the fire towards me. I panicked momentarily. Then, with a slight of movement that would have made a magician proud, I held the burning butt between my thumb and forefinger, thrusting the innocent looking cupped hand into my coat pocket in an unsuspecting way.

Intent on keeping the fire safe, the old boy wandered on by me, prodding the flaming brushwood with a stick in his efforts to check the flying sparks. I withdrew my hand and resumed my newly discovered pleasure. The cigarette, still fully alight, had burnt to within half an inch, so I took the last few puffs, then threw the smouldering butt into the bonfire.

It was then that a sudden burst of reports rattled from the confines of my coat. I knew what had happened: it was instantly obvious. In concealing the burning Woodbine in my pocket to shield it from Old Harry, the touch paper on the fireworks stored within had come in contact with the smouldering cigarette. All hell broke out, as a series of blasts and booms crackled and mingled with the hissing, spluttering, whistling and whizzing that erupted from my own little fireworks display. Again, I panicked – then in a moment whipped the illuminated garment from my back and threw it to the ground.

My brothers, mother and the old man rushed round the bonfire to see the cause of the commotion. And there we all stood, watching with a strangely amused horror the dazzling pyrotechnic display that took place as my coat was blasted to shreds. Old Harry always swore it was a stray spark from the fire that had set off the fireworks in the pocket. Who was I to argue with him?

Not many months after the exploding coat episode, the time arrived for me to leave school and find employment. With no academic qualifications, I inevitably took a job as a 'third cowman'

*Nellie Pateman in the peaceful garden
of Freehold Farm*

on a farm, helping to hand-milk a pedigree herd of Friesians. The farmer was old Algie Moss of Westlands Farm, Foxhill, Petworth.

The last day that I ever stayed in the homely old farmhouse, Freehold, has somehow remained imprinted on my mind. It was a wild, angry afternoon. The wind blew hard and there, in my room, I gazed from rain-drenched windows, fascinated by the fluid lightning that played on the ridge of Blackdown Hill. I watched for some long while. Then slowly the storm abated, and the dark clouds cleared, turning a washed yellow and setting later that evening a pure brilliant crimson. I then soon retired to my bed.

On rising the following morning, I packed my scarce few belongings in a bag, said my goodbyes to the family and strolled up the garden and out of the gate. The lengthy old lane looked as beautiful as ever. I turned, waved once again to my friends, and then drew slowly on and out of sight.

That was the last time I was to see that loveable old house for many years to come. For not long after I left home the old man gave up his job and moved to yet another place of employment.

24 The Return to Freehold

It was well over forty years since I had trodden the same ground, that old, familiar route, the woods and fields that surround the rambling farmhouse of Freehold. The lane looked much as it had always been, deep-forested through the first leg of the journey, then opening out to arable land. I wandered casually, taking in the delights of those childhood memories. It was autumn and the leaves had turned to various shades of copper. The morning sun cut wonderfully picturesque shafts of light through the seasonable mist, and I breathed in the cool luxuriant air. The pungent smell of the stink-horn fungus was strongly noticeable as I passed through that dense wood.

Soon I came out to the open fields, then on to Pheasant Court farm, where once worked Old Harry. All was quiet; nothing stirred in the animal pens. They were, without doubt, redundant. I carried on up the lane, coming in time to the bridleway that led to the dilapidated woodman's cottage. I pictured the old ruin as I wandered towards the site: the rank, musty rooms, the gaping hole in the roof, with the huge flock of white doves that had haunted the dark and lofty roof space, the picture of Jim, falling through the rotten beams. I smiled, a heavy kind of smile.

The distance through the great Wet Wood to my destination was not so far as memory had served me to believe, for before I knew it I had passed by the remnants of the garden, the plot being well disguised by the woodland trees. Nothing remained of the dwelling. It was as if it had never existed. I felt a tinge of sadness at the loss of the old place that once had such idyllic charm, but reasoned that its very remoteness must be the cause of its being rubbed from the map, just as if it were an inaccurate pencil mark.

Wandering on, I soon passed through the old fir plantation, once the habitat of the giant wood ant. What mysteries lay here, I wondered – for no more could I find those massive domed nests, so

Freehold Farm – above, in 1957; below, as it is today

finely constructed with pine needles by the ever-busy insects. What could have caused the loss of these useful ants, once so prevalent in this pine wood? There was no obvious answer.

I ambled on, soon reaching the site of the old Chaffold Mill, where, with some surprise, I took in the view before me. For there, where once spread the deep hollow of wasteland, was now a great expanse of water. It seems that in 1991 a new sluice gate had been built onto the bridge to control the water race, the sunken land then being rapidly re-flooded to form a lake. This brought the landscape back to something like it might have looked several hundred years before. Happily the ancient stone bridge, with its twin arches and ever flowing waterfall, still survived intact.

So it was that on the pond bay I rested, eyeing with a quiet pleasure the tranquil scene. The 'new' mill pond had long since settled in, harmonising with the landscape of old. Coots dallied in the reeds and a majestic swan looned idly about the motionless water, while I drank from my flask, a mug of steaming tea.

My short break over, I gathered up the thermos and ambled on, circling back and out onto the lane, then made a beeline for old Mrs Carver's cottage. The spinney where once she rode the ageing Ariel with precarious daring, looked overgrown, as if now never used. I soon reached the garden: there, before me, the plot was an impenetrable tangle of briars. I looked on in disbelief. A plantation of young trees had sprung up and over the space where once stood the cottage.

There was no point in lingering, I carried on over the tiny packhorse bridge and up through the deep, sunken lane that led to Colehook. The path had become blocked by a growth of hawthorns. I battled my way through, reaching the other end, scratched and somewhat disheartened, for this once enchanting walk was now more of an endurance test.

Cutting across a couple of fields I soon came to the Ebernoe cricket ground. The place was still the same, quiet, for ever peaceful. Pausing, I stood there a while, silently taking in the pleasing hush, and there, across the green, the mild, familiar smell of wood smoke drifted over from the manor house garden. The sweet scent brought on deeper thoughts of those childhood days – the old Horn Fair, those merry trips to the annual gathering, the hurried trek home as evening fell, our short cut through the darkening trees, accompanied part of the way by the rousing music that piped incessantly from the carousel.

Stirring from my idle day dreams, I walked leisurely on, heartened by the knowledge that this ancient fair was still held year after year. I took the same old route through the woods and on, in the direction of the isolated dwelling, Bittlesham. There I hoped to see the cottager busy in his garden and, in conversation, tell him how well I knew the place in those distant days. Climbing the steep path that led up from the common and into the open field, I looked out for the roof as the ground levelled – but nothing of the house was to be seen, or ever would be again. For it had long since been demolished, leaving no trace that it had ever been there, other than a few fragments of tile that the plough turned up each season.

The rambling farmhouse, Freehold, lay only a couple of fields away, so I hurried on, eager to again see the old place. As I drew close, it became apparent that there had been alterations. I wandered as far as the garden gate and there eyed with a stunned dismay the sorry sight. The old house, through the process of modernisation, had undergone a complete transformation. The rear door had been bricked up, with a new entrance knocked into the west face of the building. A chimney had been demolished, windows altered and the whole place spruced up, as would befit a residence more suited for the town. There appeared to have been no restraint in the alterations, no sympathy for the old-fashioned charm that was once so appealing.

The outbuildings had disappeared, as also had the great oak barn that once enclosed the cow yard. There, where once stood the cattle safely confined in the muddy enclosure, was now the crystal clear water of a swimming pool. The old timber-framed barn, I later discovered, had apparently been carefully dismantled and then, with as much care, re-erected on a site close to the village of Fittleworth, though for what reasons I know not.

My return to those old haunts reinforced my idea that, today, we live in a different world from that of my childhood. At no period in history has the destruction of our countryside – our heritage – been so great as it has during the past half-century. As a consequence a once-familiar landscape is almost beyond recognition in many places.

Change has always gone on in the land, but with a careful, obvious sympathy that ensured necessary alterations were hardly noticeable. Our forefathers, I believe, took great comfort in knowing that their children's children would inherit that same unaltered world. What loss for those who follow in our steps, who have never seen the countryside of old.

25 The Cottage on the Hill

Westlands Farm: what lucky quirk of fate allowed me the opportunity to work at this place, as opposed to a more modern dairy farm? The farmer, Algie Moss, was a character and a gentleman, one of the old breed, who doggedly refused to give up his primitive methods of farming. He still preferred to milk the cows by hand, cut the corn with a rickety, ageing binder, and each season he brought in the threshing machine to winnow the corn.

He was a short, stocky fellow, with clear blue, honest eyes and a seemingly constant smiling face. Throughout the summer and winter months his head was always covered with a flat hat that appeared to have moulded to the shape of his crown over the years. In contrast, his brawny arms were always bare because of the short-sleeved shirts and sleeveless jerseys he wore. Most times he treated his men fairly, even kindly, but woe betide the man who mistook that gentlemanly kindness for a softness in character. For he could turn fearsomely hard at the blink of an eye.

On the day that I went to the interview for the job, I stood before this 'boss' to be, feeling pleased as punch when told I could start work as soon as possible.

"Is there anywhere I can lodge while working here?" I asked, half expecting him to offer me a room in the great farmhouse.

"There's a cottage up the lane, top of the hill in the woods," he replied. "You can't miss it! It's about half a mile up there. Tell the old woman that lives there that you are to lodge with them."

"But, what if she says I can't?" I said, not feeling willing to turn up on the doorstep unannounced with such a proposal.

He lifted his flat hat with thumb and forefinger, revealing as he did so a thin, greying head of hair that he scratched vigorously as a gesture of irritation.

"You tell 'em you're to lodge with them!" he repeated in a sterner voice. "It's my cottage and if I say you're to live with them, then live with them you shall! You tell them I said so!"

"What's their name?" I asked, as I turned to go.

"White!" I heard him say, as I hurried on up the lane.

The cottage, remotely situated on the crest of Fox Hill, was the end one of a terrace of three, two of which were derelict. The old, tumble-down place, set in dense woodland, was to qualify as the coldest, most inhospitable house I have ever entered. The front door opened into a tiny, featureless room. Its stark, whitewashed walls bore down on a grey, stone slabbed floor, vacant of carpet or rugs for

The late Algie Moss of Westlands Farm

that essential comfort. A small rectangular table, with two solid wooden chairs stood against one side of the room, with a little, black range that barely gave out sufficient heat to cook a meal on the other. To the right of the main entrance a door, warped with age, opened into a dark, cupboard-sized space that was the stairwell. Above were a couple of box-sized bedrooms.

It was in this hovel that the White family spent their days, seemingly oblivious to any other better way of living. Old Mr. White, in his late sixties, was of a jovial nature, with a simple mind, typical of labourers in much older times. His wife, of similar age, was thin and very tall, with owl-like features and pure white hair, hacked off in a step level with the lobes of her ears.

She would scurry about the room, wrapped up in her own private mutterings, giving those who did not know her the impression that age had affected her mind. But I soon came to know otherwise, for she had a deep knowledge of country cures that in her kind old way came out when most required. I had not long moved in, when my hands took on an ugly growth of warts.

"Go out in the garden," she said, in her characteristically high-pitched voice. "Turn over a few stones, till you finds a white slug! Pick 'im up an' rub 'im over them warts! But don't tell anyone! And don't go washing the slime off!"

A day or two later I carried out her instructions, and within a couple of weeks all signs of the infection had disappeared.

She was, too, a hardy old stick who appeared to withstand the coldness of winter with little effect, for it was her habit to scrub the flagstone floor each day, in all seasons. The chore done, she would then leave the door fully open, allowing the ice cold air to blow dry the pools of water that had accumulated on the uneven surface. There she would sit, oblivious to the howling draughts that blew in through the gaping entrance – while I, home for my midday meal, sat and shivered the full hour in misery.

On one particular occasion, when I walked in for my dinner break, this strange old lady was sitting in her usual chair vigorously shaking a treacle tin.

"What you doing Mrs. White?" I asked in puzzled bemusement.

"Making, butter," she replied, with a wry, tight-lipped smile.

"How's that then?" I pestered.

Her answer was to pick up a well worn, steel knife to prise the lid off the container, revealing as she did so half a tin of curdled milk turning to butter. In taste, it was bland, even mildly offensive to the palette. But it was used and often at that, on our bread and jam sandwiches, the taste being well disguised by the lashings of fruity preserve spread over those doorstep slices.

It was these little, unexpected diversions that made everyday life bearable in that remote and decaying house. How well I recall those days spent working in drenching rain for the best part of the day, followed by the dismal climb up the steep path to home of an evening, saturated clothes clinging to my body. On entering those lodgings I would draw up to the fire and vacantly eye the rising steam that evaporated from the garments I wore. A sparse meal, never long in arriving, was followed an hour or two later by the routine, candlelit trudge up the stairs to the greater comfort of bed.

Rising at four in the morning, I would make my way back down the dark and sodden lane. Overhanging trees incessantly dripped in consequence of the overnight downpours, the dense canopy acting as a shield against any moonlight. In this condition, the pitch black path was always blindly negotiated without a torch, each step presupposing a familiarity with the route. When drawing close to my place of work, the old house, barns and outbuildings would just be made out, a dark silhouette in the dim light of dawn.

On those cold winter mornings it was always a relief to reach the farm, to hurry across the cow yard and disappear into the more favourable temperatures of the cow sheds. It was surprising how warm the body heat from those bovine beasts kept the place overnight. Confined to the sheds during the winter months, the herd contentedly chewed their cud during the dark hours, patiently waiting each milking session.

26 The Art of Hand-milking

That morning, when first I began the job, I scurried down the lane and into the cow shed bright and early. There, waiting my presence, was Algie Moss.

"Hello lad," he said, his face beaming at my prompt arrival. "All settled in up at the Whites' place then?"

"Yes! Yes, all's o.k. up there," I assured him.

"Good! Well, these are the milkers you're to look after," he continued, waving an arm in the general direction of half a dozen cows that stood in a row.

The first in the line he patted on the flank with his great brawny hand. It was a placid, weary looking animal.

"C'mon, move over old girl," he coaxed. The docile beast flinched its hide, but barely moved, while he, the kindly governor, nodded his head in the general direction of a bucket and stool close by.

"See how you get on with her," he said encouragingly.

I squatted awkwardly astride the seat, and listened with an eager ear to the few tips of advice that he passed on about hand-milking.

"You'll soon pick it up now," he again encouraged, then wandered off to the far end of the cowshed.

"If you get into difficulty, Thompson will help you," he hollered back over his shoulder.

Jack Thompson was the head dairyman. He looked up from beneath the cow he milked a little further up the row and smiled, a broad toothless smile. At one time, in his younger days, he might have been a good looking fellow, tall with dark wavy hair and angelic features. But time and toil had wearied the man, leaving no more than a hint of his former looks, his youthful days.

A couple of weeks later I had got into the swing of things, milking that team of cows with the skill of an old hand. Well, so I thought – but how wrong I was. For in strolled Thompson, bold as you like one morning, with stool in one hand, bucket in the other.

"The'll have to speed up more'n that boy!" he wheezed, his thin, hoary lips clutching the end of a cigarette like a miniature vice.

"How'd you mean, Jack?" I replied, a little staggered by his suggestion.

"Too slow! Too slow!" he moaned. "You need to keep the jet of milk a-flowing boy. You see, you ain't milking the beast prop'ly till you've got a good head of froth on the milk like that of a pint of beer!"

"Is that so?" I said. "Then I'll have to try harder."

Several days had passed before I had acquired sufficient skill to be rewarded with a creamy head of froth that topped the milk in the bucket. But that was not the only tip the wise old cowman was to pass on to me, for he had one more trick up his sleeve that proved of constant value in the task of milking by hand. It was again early morning and I was a couple of cows into the session when, without warning, the animal I milked lifted her foot and booted me, the stool and bucket into the manure gully. There I lay, sprawled out beneath the rear end of the beast, covered in muck. The milk, too, had spilled from the bucket and ran down the drain, like a tawny cream sauce.

Old Thompson, a cow or two further up the line, chuckled.

"Tee! Hee! Come a cropper then, boy?" he teased.

My pride was hurt and I felt a little annoyed, but could see the funny side of it so laughed along with the old fellow's sadistic humour.

"What'd she doo lad?" he carried on. "Up wid her foot an' put it in the bucket?"

"Yes!" I replied with a feeble laugh. "She took me by surprise!"

"There's a way of stoppin' that ya knows!" he said with a more serious note. "Rest your forehead onto cows flank, just in front of the top of her leg! You'll soon tell then when she's goin' ta kick! You'll feel 'er flinch. An' besides, if'n you press hard with your head into cow's groin like that, it hurts 'em to kick you. They soon learns you know!"

"Does it work every time?" I ventured.

"Noo!" He admitted. "Thar's some cows as is determined to kick you! No matter what you does!"

So it was that with these small snippets of bovine husbandry, passed on to me by the old dairyman, I in time became proficient in the art of hand-milking – although I still occasionally came a cropper as a result of the odd cow that let fly with a hoof when least expected.

Yet, I counted my blessings. For the governor, old Algie, always took on the most disagreeable beasts, the highly strung animals that were tethered in a separate shed for that very reason. How often was I startled by the sound of his cursing, a result of some poor beast that had toppled him from the milking stool during that precarious task.

The high volume of words that suddenly erupted on those occasions always seemed out of character with the normally placid nature of the man. They often drew me from my work, to venture into that cow stall to discover the cause of the violent outburst.

It was not unusual to see the milk awash on the cowshed floor, the governor plastered in muck, yet not beaten. For he would have at hand a strong rick rope that he always used to lash the beast's hind feet together. He would then run out the cord to a steel bull-ring fastened on the wall to the rear of the animal. With the rope tied to this metal anchor, it was impossible for the animal to kick. Yet strangely, for all this treatment, those few very nervous cows somehow never changed their ways. They were as constant in their contrary nature as the boss was in his determination to break them of it.

With the morning milking sessions over, we would wash the buckets, scrub the dairy, sterilise the cooler and then roll out the churns for collection by the milk lorry. This done, there was then the daily routine of mucking out and washing down the cow sheds. The dung was always carted to the fields, where Algie expected his men to manually spread the manure with the use of a dung fork. There was never any mention of bringing in a mechanical muck spreader to carry out this task.

How strangely old-fashioned the governor had remained, in view of the fact that he farmed in earnest, not for pleasure. As the world moved on and agriculture progressed, he held fast to his tried and tested methods of working the land. I well recall the day he asked me to help with the task of 'mole-draining'. The contraption he used for the job, was I believe, of Victorian invention – a museum relic.

There we were, perched on the side of a steep field, an ancient Ford Standard tractor with iron spiked wheels parked at a distance, on the lowest level of the escarpment. We fiddled and fought with the mole-drainer to set it right– a bolt pulled tight here, a nut there; the iron rope adjusted, flipped this way, then that; while old Algie lifted his hat a dozen times to scratch his balding patch in exasperation. Then finally –- "That's it boy!" he said with a look of satisfaction. "I think it's about right now."

I eyed the weird and wondrous machine with some doubt that it would ever work. In appearance it resembled the dagger board of a small sailing craft, with a foot-long torpedo-shaped object fastened on the lower edge of the blade. The whole device was securely connected to a metal cable that stretched down the field to a pulley located at the rear of the tractor.

"Right ho, lad. Nip down there and get the tractor to wind in the rope," commanded the boss.

It took minutes to reach the throbbing engine. I manipulated a lever and the sagging iron rope came tight, juddered, then began to pull the mole drain down the hill. I watched it sink into the earth, like the tips of a plough, then gradually heave towards me, boring a continuous, subterranean hole in its course.

Throughout the day we repeated this task, each drain being a dozen or so feet distant from the other. With the drawing in of evening, Old Algie remarked how satisfied he was with the job, and he endlessly praised the antiquated machine as we made our way back to the farm.

27 Gathering Fruit

As the year drew on, the hot summer days soon turned the corn sufficiently to herald the beginning of harvest. The ageing binder was then pulled from the shelter of the cart shed, cleaned, repaired, and the serrated blades sharpened to a razor edge. All was then deemed ready to start the cutting.

The tractor heaved the machine steadily out to the field, Algie in the driving seat, Jack Thompson riding the binder. I followed the rickety procession on foot, the morning sun already warm on my face. There I watched as they cut a course round the headland. Then with the first sheaves cast in a row, I began the stooking, and so the day wore on, the old binder chattering gloriously in never ending circles.

Come late afternoon that dependable old machine gave up the ghost. The engine of the tractor was cut and all fell silent. Both men jumped to the ground. How well I bring to mind the old fashioned scene that followed, as I stretched my eyes from a distant corner of the field – two men of the soil, their heads tucked into the bowels of the broken apparatus in their efforts to discover the fault; their voices drifting over in diluted tones, words indistinct; the corn waving in the gentle breeze; the old labourer now buried beneath the vintage binder, while the governor mops his brow with hat raised in one hand, kerchief in the other; then the ringing of metal on metal as a vital component is hammered into place; and the satisfied looks as they again fall to their work.

There I watched for some while the slow, rhythmic progress of harvest, those sporadic flurries of dust turned up with the sails of the binder, the incessant chatter of the cutting blades and the multitudes of rabbits that scurried from the cover of standing corn on the approach of the noisy machine – in all a picture of 'olde England' I will always treasure.

It was then, while looking over that peaceful scene, that I first caught a glimpse of a figure hurrying down the farm lane. It was a man of burly stature. I watched him enter the garden and stride up to the farmhouse. The front door opened, there was a pause, then he turned and made a beeline for the governor in the harvest field. There the tractor was brought to a halt and a conversation took place, the topic of which culminated in the hiring of the man as a third cowman on the farm. It was an action which, in time, was to affect me more than I could have supposed when first I saw this labouring giant.

The harvest came to an end, autumn turned the corner, and apple picking was in full swing. The sizeable orchard lay at the back of the farmhouse, the fruit trees coming up to within a few feet of the rear door. Here, great wicker baskets, some full to the brim, were scattered about the greensward that served as the lawn. It was a gloriously warm, autumn day and the boss worked alongside his labourers. We all gathered in the crop at our own, unhurried pace.

"Can you go and get the rick ladder, Jack?" the old governor asked. "And get Arthur to help you. It's lying down, alongside the cart shed."

Arthur Baines was the newly recruited third cowman. He followed Thompson across the farmyard in search of the wooden structure. Soon they reappeared, the enormously long ladder balanced unevenly between them. Their contrasting figures were the more noticeable as they worked together. The hoary dairyman, Jack, tall and thin, was in the lead, while Arthur Baines, built like an ox, was bringing up the rear. They simultaneously slipped the contraption from their shoulders onto the open patch of ground. I eyed it warily, for it appeared worm-eaten, with evidence of makeshift repairs along the shafts and some of the rungs.

"Where do ya want it put, governor?" asked Thompson, his chest heaving and wheezing in its efforts to recover from those few minutes' exertion.

"Put 'im up on that tree there," replied Algie, pointing to a bulky apple tree that had grown to a considerable height.

"Set it up safe," he continued. "And you'd better let the boy go up there. He's the lightest."

The foolish daring of youth got the better of my judgement and I readily went along with the governor's wishes. I climbed carelessly, the safety support reaching over twenty feet in height. Nearing the top-most treads, I leant over to grasp the ripest fruit. There was no warning that anything was wrong – all of a sudden the worn-out device snapped and I fell instantly, landing heavily on my back. I lay there fully winded, the governor and his fellow workers peering down at me.

"You all right lad?" asked Algie.

I looked up at the three faces that all appeared a sickly white and mumbled, "Yes, I think so!"

The pain was virtually unbearable.

Happily nothing was broken and, although feeling stiff, I was back at work the next morning. I vowed, though, never again to trust any of old Algie's antiquated tools and farm equipment without first giving such apparatus a thorough safety inspection.

28 The Labouring Giant Picks a Fight

A few weeks later and threshing was in progress. The great machine hummed away the hours, belching billows of dust that smothered the men as they toiled throughout each day. Somehow I had managed to escape the grime-ridden task by being nominated as tractor driver by the governor. There I sat, proudly perched on the old Fordson, patiently waiting the loading of the corn sacks onto the trailer. The first load done, I started the engine and steadily transported the bagged grain to the granary. On route, I met the old rustic, Thompson, coming in from the fields, a dung fork he held indicating the task he had just finished. I gave him a wave. He returned the greeting with his toothless smile, and then carried on across the yard to join the busy band of men that worked the machine. Slowly, I drove on towards the barn, scattering a few chickens as I passed between them. How wonderfully busy the old farm appeared, always a constant hive of activity, a thriving industry.

The beefy giant, Arthur Baines, along with one of the men from the thrashing team, carried the great two-and-a-quarter hundredweight sacks from the trailer to the corn store. The burly ox tossed a bag on to his shoulder and virtually ran up the half-dozen granary steps, returning in minutes for another.

"C'mon, boy. Ain't you going to give a hand? Or you gonna sit a-top that tractor all day?" he grumbled.

"Gov'nor said the sacks are too much for me to carry. That's why I'm driving the tractor," I protested.

"Dooh! Young lad like you! Boy, when I was your age, I'd have lifted more'n those bags weigh!"

"Well, I'll give it a try." I replied, as I leapt down from the vehicle and strode round to the rear of the cart.

The great sack was shuffled onto my back by the threshing team labourer, and I staggered towards the staddle barn. The dead weight of the confined grain, double my weight, made me wander like a drunk up the series of steps. On reaching the door, I bolted forward and shot the bagged contents into the corn bin. It was painful, but I was not beaten. I returned for another, if only as proof that the carrying of the first was no fluke. The job done, I climbed back onto the tractor, and there I stayed as driver for the remainder of the threshing period.

Winter had come and gone, and the lighter days of Spring made the trek to work in the mornings less of an ordeal. I bustled about the cowshed, busily preparing the animals for the milking session. Ten minutes later Arthur Baines turned up. He barged in through the door like an angry bull, strutted the full length of the cow shed, and then bawled menacingly back to me.

"You sin my matches, boy?"

I looked up a little startled.

"No I've not seen them!" I said. "I've got my own. Here you can borrow them to light your fag!"

"I don't want yours! I want the box I left here last night. They were up on that window sill," he raved.

Not caring to be drawn further into the argument, I turned away from the man's bellowing and got on with the more important task of preparing to milk the cows. I stooped to pick up the bucket and stool, and then straightened my back. As I did so, I caught in the corner of my eye the shadow of the hefty ox bearing down on me. His trunk-like limbs crushed me against the wall. I tried to escape, but it was no use, he wrapped a massive hand around my throat and held me rigid.

"Now tell me you ain't got my matches, boy!" he roared.

His great fist tightened about my windpipe. I panicked, twisting my head to one side and his grip loosened. I took my chance, ducking down in an instant, then slipped from under his arms, raced up the length of the cowstall and out through the door to the yard. There, I met old Algie, whistling his way in to work. His engaging tune soon ceased, as he eyed me with some surprise, rushing from the milking shed in frantic alarm.

"What's the matter lad?" he asked.

"That man Baines, just attacked me!" I panted.

Then, with renewed breath, I went on to explain what had taken place.

The governor's normally placid features took on a sternness that I had not before seen. He strode towards the cowshed.

"I'll see him about this!" he growled as he disappeared through the entrance. I followed close behind.

"What's the meaning of pushing the boy about?" he stormed. "If you want to know who took your bloody matches, I did! Now what you going to do about that?"

The burly giant looked down with the meek expression of a lamb. He remained speechless as old Algie raged on.

"If you want to throw your bloody weight about, then throw it at me," he said. "Any more of it and you'll be out the door and up the road!"

Old Baines nodded his head silently, then slunk back to the task of milking. Thereafter, like a shadow, he moved about the farm doing his daily chores with barely a word passing his lips. The incident was never again mentioned. We rarely spoke, other than a nod or grunt when occasion compelled some form of communication relative to our work.

The once easy going, happy environment, always so apparent about the farm, had been destroyed in an instant. The strained relations that inevitably followed rapidly festered, making working conditions intolerable. Within two months, I handed in my notice, having first obtained a new position as a cowman at Juppsland Farm, a dairy farm in the village of Adversane, close to Billingshurst.

29 The Return to Westlands

As I puffed my way up the steep woodland path, I wondered at the toll life takes on the body in the passing of half a century. For, as I climbed, I recalled the ease with which I had taken the same route in those far off teenage years. The everyday comings and goings from Westlands to the isolated house on the hill I then considered nothing, in spite of the long hours of agricultural toil.

Glimpses of the dwelling could be seen through the dense foliage, as I neared the summit. I was surprised it still survived. I paused for breath, and then ambled on till the old place came full in to view. How different it appeared! The three cottages had been knocked into one and caringly restored, along with the gardens – now a single, well-cultivated plot. Flowering shrubs and sweeping lawns had matured to a lush splendour, portraying a picture of affluence. The place had apparently been sold when Algie Moss retired in 1974 along with his beloved Westlands.

I turned and made my way back down the path to look over the old farm. It was springtime, and the woodland birds were in fine tune. I walked leisurely beneath the canopy of trees that sheltered the track. There in the glades I noticed the carpets of wild daffodils still covering the forest floor, to captivate the eye of the wanderer as they did long ago. Soon I reached the open lane that winds a course down to Westlands. Primroses still adorned the mossy banks that flanked the byway, with here and there pleasing daubs of celandine to vary the pastel shades along the route. The old lane, I was pleased to note, still held onto its enduring charm.

The great farmhouse with its cluster of barns looked from a distance unaltered. But as I drew close, a curious quietness became apparent. The once familiar sounds about the old farm buildings had gone: an eerie silence lingered. There I stood in the shadow of the old cow-stall, listening. Across the yard the great barn door shuddered in the squall of a sudden breeze. I looked up, distracted by the momentary disturbance, then resumed my silent observations. No more could I hear the busy clatter of churns or the earthy voices of old Algie and his men who frequently persuaded stubborn beasts to "be still" or "move over old girl" in the daily course of milking. The bustle of the dairyman's employment had long since ceased. The buildings, once overlooked through overwork, were now neglected and decayed through idleness.

30 Juppsland Farm, Adversane

Juppsland, once a thriving farm, was by the time I worked there no more than a shadow of its former importance. Separated from the village and highway by a small field, the old place was made up of the great barn, milking shed and dairy. There was a tiny cow yard, a few pig pens and a rick yard with several acres of meadowland beyond, where roamed the dairy herd.

The once great farm house had been severed from the farm under the terms of a ninety-nine year lease, the farmer, Miss Dryden, living then in the only tied cottage that remained. She was a woman of middle age with a fiercely independent nature that compelled her to run the farm virtually single-handed. There was though, a price to pay for this strenuous method of living, for the constant burden of maintaining the place, the general labouring, tractor driving and the feeding of the livestock had taken its toll.

Her hair always appeared an untidy mass, lying in dark, matted locks over her leathery face. The everyday clothes she wore never differed in design or colour. Threadbare, torn and smeared with the inevitable grime picked up about the farm, her jerseys and heavy brown cords were as much a part of her character as her well-weathered features. She too had strange ways.

A day or two after I had started the job she drove into the cow-yard with her old car, a 1938 MG convertible. It misfired and spluttered to a halt by the great barn door. I was just crossing the yard at the time and looked up in surprise at her noisy arrival.

"Get me a couple of bales of hay and put them in the car for me, David," she said as she swung a leg up and over the door of the vehicle and climbed out.

I threw a couple of bales into the passenger seat, then stood there looking on at the old motor. The wire wheels were rusty and caked with mud, splats of cow manure covered the fading blue paintwork and the doors were held in place by binding string. I stared in disbelief at the sad neglect. The leather seats and walnut dashboard looked tired and weather-beaten, there being ,I noticed, no hood to protect the interior during the wet winter months.

"Lovely car," I said as she climbed back into the vehicle and pressed the starter.

"Yes," she replied "it's getting a little worn out now though."

She then spun the rattling vehicle round and rumbled back out of the yard, the two bales poking skywards in the passenger seat, her hair and jersey covered in seed, a trail of hay spilling out in her wake.

In spite of her odd ways she was a kind and caring boss, for she readily decided that I should stay with her in the same cottage, as her lodger. The dwelling, separated from the farm by the village, necessitated the short walk each day down the main street, past the blacksmith's, by the pub, then up the short lane to the farm yard. There my duties involved the machine-milking of a pedigree herd of around thirty Jerseys, a responsible job that I took seriously from the start, ensuring the welfare of the animals in every respect. This involved preparing the correct measurements of food, looking out for milk infections such as mastitus and the important task of keeping an account of the daily quota of milk produced by each cow. The very nature of my employment was to me a constant inspiration. It was, for sure, a love affair with the countryside I lived in, a deep affection for the quiet, unhurried world I had grown up in since leaving those city streets of years gone by.

In my comings and goings to and from work my eyes were occasionally drawn to the open doors and the inner sanctum of the blacksmith's shop. There I would notice, in passing, a few of the old rustics gathered in a group within, chatting and guffawing their autumn days away. At other times, the busy ring of hammer on anvil would attract my attention. I would then poke my nose into the lively shadows where the familiar figure toiled, watching the glowing shape of the man slaving by the furnace, his venerable companions looking on, as if mesmerised by the skill of their age-old friend. A few cheerful words would pass between us, and then I would make my way back out and on towards my work.

When first I looked into that busy chamber, I was greeted by the old smithy with a broad smile.

"You must be the new cowman up at Dryden's place?" he chuckled with a cautious note.

"Yes!" I assured him.

His old and decrepit companion, who stood by looking on, cackled as if he understood the suppressed laugh of his industrious friend.

"She don't hang on to her staff long, you know!" the old blacksmith continued.

"No, no more'en she looks after her animals either," put in the other old rustic. "Look at the time her cowman got roughed up by 'er bull. Mauled him purty bad ya know!"

The sweating smithy stepped over to his furnace, jabbed the metal rod he was working on into the fire, then pumped the bellows furiously.

"Mind you, I don't think she purposely neglects her livestock, you know. She just don't 'ave a clue how to look after animals," he said, still jerking at the bellows.

Not wishing to upset the two old companions by saying something contrary to their views, I laughed a short, hesitant laugh, as if in agreement with their sentiments. This had the effect of momentarily cramping the good humoured chatter.

After a short pause, the old smithy piped up again.

"She used to have an old pig, you know, that she had brought up from a suckling," he said. "She'd walk it about the village tethered on a bit of rope, jest as if it were a dog."

Both men guffawed mockingly as they recalled the comical scene.

"Yes, she's a rum 'un, of that there's no doubt!" put in the blacksmith's elderly friend. "Do ya mind the time she had that old piebald pony – must be a good few years back now?"

"Yes, yes I do. She kept 'im in that old meadow by the road," interrupted the smithy. "They say she got 'im from a circus, 'cos when the band played outside the pub he'd rear up on his hind legs and dance round the field to the music."

Again the two men laughed loudly while I smiled and mused over the story. It seemed a little too far-fetched to me, so following the jocular outburst that the reminiscences had caused, I tackled them over it, saying that they were surely pulling my leg.

"No," they said. "Anyone in the village will tell you the same. They all know's it's true."

With this I wandered out of the forge, still smiling at the very thought of the amusing tales told to me so vividly by this venerable and well-known rustic of the village. For he was none other than the celebrated Gaius Carley, whose tales of old smithing days took the listeners back to the 1890s when he was a child.

The memoirs that he wrote down in the mid-Fifties were eventually published a few years later, throwing light on the fact that his great stock of stories must have provided unending entertainment for that circle of venerable friends who always lingered about the old blacksmith's shop.

31 The Gypsy Camp

No more than three or four weeks had passed since I had first taken the job, when one afternoon I was surprised by the appearance in the cowshed of a lad about my own age. He was of average height, with fair, curly hair, blue eyes and a mischievous smile.

"We've parked our van in the field," he blurted out. "So we needs a couple of buckets of water."

"Does Miss Dryden know you're there?" I asked.

"Yes," he replied, his smile broadening to display a fine row of well-set teeth. "She said it was o.k!"

I waved a hand in the general direction of the dairy and told him to take whatever water he required. He scurried off to the taproom, noisily clanged the buckets about and then disappeared.

Later, when I had finished the milking session, I wandered out to the little field by the road. There, close to the dividing hedge, was parked an old gypsy caravan. The young lad who had called in on his water-collecting errand loafed with feet outstretched on the steps of the vehicle. His family lay sprawled about the grass close by.

They were all in high spirits, the younger children bursting into uncontrollable giggles as they leapt up to chase each other, frolicking in circles and then falling again to the ground. I watched them for some minutes, counting seven altogether in the group. There were three girls and two boys, ranging in age from around six or seven up to twenty-three or -four. The parents looked far too old to have such young members in their clutch. The father fitted the description more suited to a grandfather, his face dark and swarthy, with deeply-creased features and a great brown stained bushy moustache. He was surely the chief of all gypsies. I slipped back to the cool dairy, without being noticed, and then made my way back home.

Over the ensuing weeks I came to know that band of travellers well, their traipsing to and fro for fresh water being the perfect means of introduction to all members of the family. There were often times when one or the other took it into their head to use the farm buckets for their water-carrying escapades. On such occasions I would trek over to their camp to retrieve the receptacle, finding a good excuse for any amount of conversation, which often included snippets about their way of life.

One particular day, when wandering over to their settlement, I happened to notice one of the daughters, a girl in her early teens, busily stringing up a necklace of tiny shells. It had been a warm day in late spring, and she lay stretched out on the greensward close by the van. Her nimble fingers worked the needle and thread through the minute orifice and brittle case of each delicate mollusc to create the most intricate design I had ever seen. I commented on how pretty the well-strung collar looked.

Smiling sweetly, she held up the unfinished article to show me, her eyes beaming with pride as she announced that it was a present for her little sister.

"Who taught you to make such intricate bead-work as that then, Emily?" I asked.

"Me Mam," she replied. "We picks up the shells wherever we finds 'em, up along the way. You knows, as we goes to different places 'an all."

"Who taught your mother then?" I delved.

"Dunno! 'Er mum I 'spect! Anyhow, she can make 'em better'n I can."

Her eyes fell back to the intricately woven necklace, to again take up the tedious task, while I retrieved my dairy pails from the undercarriage of the van and made my way back to the farm.

Another time, when on a similar errand, I fell into conversation with Phil, the lad of my own age. We had not been chatting long before his elder brother George marched over in our direction, saying as he approached that his dad wanted to talk to him about something.

"What's he want?" asked Phil.

The reply that George made was clearly not for my ears, for they spoke in a language that had neither meaning or understanding. Their words were brief, and when they had finished, Phil resorted back to English, saying that he would go in directly to see his father.

"What sort of language is that?" I asked.

Phil smiled in that mischievous way.

"Oh, it's a kind of back slang," he replied. "You see, you take the letter from the back of each word, put it to the front and talk like that. Its easy!"

I puzzled over it for a minute or two.

"Give it a try," he urged, as he turned and hurried off towards the caravan, saying over his shoulder as he went that he would be back in a few minutes.

During the time he was gone I 'gave it a try ', coming very soon to the conclusion that what he had told me was rubbish. Try as I might, the words made up in the way he had described were impossible to form into verbal syllables. When he returned I challenged him, saying that it made no sense. He looked at first a little sheepish, and then his smile broadened momentarily, turning soon to a silent, knowing grin, as if to say "It's for me to know, and you to guess!" I felt our recently formed friendship had been unfairly snubbed by the refusal to share the knowledge of that mysterious tongue, the secret of which I never did discover.

Strangely, although one door to that old gypsy tradition was barred to me, I was about to enter through another thanks to the privilege of an unexpected invitation. For Phil's maddeningly smug grin soon faded, when the reason for having to see his father surfaced.

"Me Dad's gotta go knife-grinding tomorrow," he said. "And George an' me generally gives 'im an' 'and. But we're both busy, so we can't. He wants to know if you would go along with him."

A ripple of excitement ran through me at such a proposal, for I knew how rare the occurrence was for an outsider to join in the often shrouded ways of any band of travelling gypsies.

"Well, yes." I replied. "I can take the day off and go with him. What will he want me to do?"

"Oh! not much. Keep the stone wet an' keep it turning while he does the grinding," the gypsy boy replied.

"You'll be going in that!" he continued, pointing with a swift gesture of the hand to a rusting old motor van parked up beside the caravan. The vehicle belonged to the eldest son, George, though it seemed to have been shared by any member of the family when needs most required its use.

The following morning, not long after dawn, I climbed into the veteran vehicle, the ruling gypsy in the driving seat. Soon we were on the road. I hoped for conversation, but the miles strangely passed in silence. Here and there, along the country lanes, we pulled in beside affluent houses where the old gypsy found a fair amount of work. Shears, clippers, scissors, knives, in fact tools of all description were carried out at one time or another, to come under his sharpening skills.

"Keep wetting the stone," he would say. "Keep wetting the stone," while I splashed water from a tin container held in one hand and turned the grindstone with the other.

The morning passed in a slow, yet oddly methodical way, the chores undertaken having a peculiar calming effect that I had not before experienced. My elderly companion rarely spoke more than an isolated sentence or two. His solemn mood was somehow more inspirational to passive thoughts than uneasy feelings at those prolonged stages of silence. The few words spoken were never wasted; each had a valid reason. There was, in addition to his cool, quiet nature, a noticeable wisdom that must have been the impetus for such persistence in withdrawing from the traditional, bustling world. He was for sure, a silent, ageing spirit, fully at one with the quieter, steady life of a Romany gypsy.

"We'd best get some grub on the go," he said, as he drew the vehicle to a halt close by a patch of woodland. He wandered into the shade of the trees, and I followed on his heels. There we gathered a few dry sticks that were thrown wigwam style over crumpled newspaper. A match set the kindling ablaze and in less than five minutes great chunks of bacon sizzled in a pan over the flames. The wood smoke filtered through the copse, like the lingering mist of an autumn morning. We squatted contentedly by the warming fire, where there I sank my teeth into doorstep slices, surely the most scrumptious bacon sandwich I had ever tasted, all cooked to delicious perfection!

That afternoon passed similar to the first half of the day, the abundance of work keeping us busy until the sun fell low in the sky. We rumbled into the tiny meadow and pulled up to the rear of the caravan, the old traveller mumbling a few words of gratitude for the day's work done. I faltered, a moments hesitation, for I expected to be paid in return for that "well appreciated" casual day's graft. But it was not to be. The crafty old knife-grinder climbed out of the vehicle, bid a swift farewell with a wave of his hand and disappeared into the shelter of the covered wagon.

I wandered off to my lodgings with the idea that "He may well pay me tomorrow!" But what false hope that was to prove. In the days that followed he made no effort to put his hand in his pocket. I resented the loss, for I had spent a whole day grinding and wetting the stone for what turned out to be no return in silver. It was a hard lesson that I have often wondered may well have been the purpose of the wise old gypsy – to teach me the foolishness of not agreeing payment prior to a day's work.

There was, though, an odd form of reward, in that I now seemed more closely accepted into the circle of their normally forbidding Romany camp. It was a great privilege for a conventional outsider.

32 A Fatal Disease in the Cows

One afternoon, during the milking session, I happened to notice a certain deterioration in the health of half-a-dozen cows. I made a point of keeping an eye on them. Several weeks past by and those animals grew worse, becoming eventually emaciated and run down. No matter how well I fed them, there was no improvement. I inevitably notified the governor, Miss Dryden, who responded by calling out the vet. He took a number of tests, went away and then returned a day or two later with the results. Five animals were diagnosed with 'Johne's Disease', a form of paratuberculosis. They had it seems, picked up the ailment by drinking bad water in the fields.

"There's no cure for this disorder," the vet said, "so all the beasts with the infection will have to be destroyed."

I was devastated by the very thought of such drastic actions, for in the role of dairyman I had grown fond of those reliable, placid beasts. I had come to know each by name during the everyday routine of milking: Daisy, Bluebell, Buttercup, Rose, Violet and numerous other titles of a similar kind were used to make up the herd, each individual animal being easily identifiable by its own distinctive markings. There is no doubt that during my constant management I had, perhaps foolishly, come to regard them more as domestic pets than farm animals – a weakness so often suffered by those who work in prolonged shifts with animals of any description.

There were, too, those few special beasts which stood out among the others for their quiet, unhurried nature, their obvious trust in the dairyman who hovered around the cowsheds, forever busy with the necessary chores. It was, for sure, impossible to work with those animals without feeling some affection for them.

That merciless day soon came round. The slaughter-house lorry arrived on time, parking conveniently in the yard, while those five cows happily chewed the cud in the cowshed, unknowingly awaiting their end.

"OK! Lets be having them," ordered the slaughter man.

I braced myself, having resolved to show no possible signs of emotion. Then, from the dairy door, I marched into the shed and up to the first beast, released the chain that tethered her and led that tame old milker out to the yard. She looked at me with her trusting eyes, placid as ever. My stomach tightened, knotted to a sickening grip. I looked away. The humane gun, placed on her forehead, went off. The yard echoed with the thunder clap of the live shot: the treacherous bolt was driven home. I turned to face the animal in that barbarous moment. Her bright eyes sparkled no longer; she saw me no more. In an instant her legs gave way, and all life expired. I wiped that damning tear from the cheeks of my face and strode back into the cowshed to bring out the next poor brute. One after another the five beasts were annihilated, each scene being a repeat of the first.

No more did I ever want to go through that again. That evening I gave in my notice to quit the job, vowing I would never again work with animals, swearing that I would never again take part in such barbarous slaughter. No matter what justifiable cause there might be for the case, I was not the man for the task. Within a month I had left the farm for ever, taking up in its place an engineering apprenticeship in the suburbs of a southern town.

The old farm at Adversane has now long since gone, as too has the tiny field where camped the family of Romany gypsies. There, replacing the farm buildings and that patch of green space, are now a number of posh houses – spick, span and giving the impression of a brand new housing complex, yet still going by the name of Juppsland Farm.

33 A Return to Country Lanes

So it was that I determined to leave the farm for good, never to return. But the draw of the land proved too strong in the end. By the early eighties I yearned to wander again those old country lanes, the open fields, the great South Downs. I had, though, no inkling at the time of the shock that awaited me on that return. The immense change that had taken place in the countryside in that half century was unexpected. It left me numb.

Where, I wondered, were all the skylarks, those thrilling songsters of the open air? I missed too, the haunting cry of plovers that were always so abundant in the ploughed fields of winter. Then again, while walking the green lanes, I puzzled at the loss of butterflies, the hordes of different species that skipped about the hedgerows. I noted, too, that the once common burnet moth was now rarely seen. I dearly missed all these things and more.

What was it, I wondered, that had contributed to this profound change? The reasons were not always immediately obvious. Indications came in dribs and drabs, as was the case a couple of months back when I was invited to go along to a ploughing match that was marking its centenary by a dinner, attended by some notable dignitaries and high-ranking farmers. I had gone along to take a few photos as a record of the occasion.

The farmhouse and barns that belonged to the landowner hosting the event stood on high ground with captivating views looking down a valley of old-fashioned parkland. The massive field where the numerous contestants ploughed their allotted strips stretched out a considerable distance from this farm.

It was over that busy piece of ground that a farming friend and I ambled, both of us admiring the enthusiasm that the event had drawn.

"It's nice to see so many old and different types of tractors still working in these days," I commented.

"Yes!" he said, smiling broadly. "And don't the heavy horses look good, too?"

We stood there for a moment, silently taking in the old-world charm of the steady work that was taking place before us, the snorting shires tugging their plough, the vintage tractor heaving its three-furrow contraption through the soil.

"Do you know," said my friend, with a note of regret in his voice, "that ploughing is now becoming a thing of the past?"

"No! I didn't," I replied, startled at the news. "Why's that then?"

"Well! They only scratches the top three inches of the ground now. They uses a kind of cultivator, you knows! You see, they don't put manure over the ground like they used to! So there's no need to turn the soil over, to turn in the muck, 'cos there ain't none spread on the land to turn in!"

"Oh! I see," I said. "That explains why the ground about here is so sandy. It's almost like a desert in some places!"

"Yes!" the old farmer laughed cynically. "Do you know, thar's about a hundred acres out there in this one field, and not a damn worm in any of it!"

"I can believe that!" I replied. "For at one time there used to be a flock or two of seagulls following the plough for bait. But there's none out there today. There's not a bird in sight!"

"No! And there ain't never likely to be, all the time things stay as they are!" he grumbled.

"Well, why don't they spread some cow manure over the fields? That'll do the ground some good!" I suggested.

"They can't," he moaned. " 'Cos they ain't got none! One time o' day, as you well know yer'self, every farm had a dairy herd. But it got like that where it didn't pay to keep 'em. So they sold their animals and turned to other ways of farming. And there we are. No livestock, no dung and a few years later the fields look like this, patches of sandy desert!"

"Yes!" I said. "It's a hard blow for farming, and a worse one for the countryside."

On arriving home that day I felt angry and frustrated that farmers had been driven to a point at which they had no option but to allow the land in most parts to fall barren around them. That soil, now void of all goodness, had in years gone by sustained life for many hundreds of species of wild flowers – flora that had been the perfect habitat for an abundance of wildlife since time immemorial. If there was ever a case for bringing back the old way of farming then this was it, I concluded: herds of dairy and beef cattle grazing the meadows, great heaps of manure to cart out to the fields, enriching the soil for the good of the farmer and the land. After all, it was the hundreds of years of traditional farming that gave us the land we all love so much to admire.

Not too long ago I ambled down a track that passed through a once-prosperous farm. The barns and farm buildings lay silent, solemn in their death throes, the cow-yard a tangle of briars, the milking parlour eerily quite. Nothing stirred. There was, in wandering about these sad, tumble-down structures an uncomfortable emptiness, a silence so intense that they gave the impression of shouting a soul-destroying scream – as if crying out for some purpose; for perhaps some use again as agricultural buildings.

I photographed, as a record, the cluster of barns to add to my growing archive, then came away and resumed my walk. But there lingered in me for some period of time a disturbing feeling of loss, similar to that felt on the morning following the Great Storm of 1987. It was as if I had been deprived of that to which I was entitled – my heritage, my right to see the land about me unaltered, as I knew it when I was a boy, still looking as it had been of old.

Later that day, crossing a field, I happened to meet an elderly farmer whom I had known for some years. He was out surveying his land in his Land Rover, as farmers have a habit of doing. He pulled up beside me and we soon got into conversation, the topic leading swiftly round to the dilapidated farm I had seen earlier and the noticeable deterioration in the countryside in general.

"The fall of one seems to be naturally bringing down the other," we both agreed.

"It makes you wonder where it will all end," I continued.

"Yes!" he replied. "But do you know, I strongly believe that farming in the old way, the way that we knew it, will one day return! Of that I'm certain!"

"Is it ever possible?" I said.

He smiled at my rhetorical remark, then put his foot gently on the accelerator, mumbling as he did so that he "must get on."

The vehicle drew slowly away, and I watched him rumble across the field. His conviction that farming in the old way would one day return lingered in my mind, but whether or not that proved an accurate prediction, I concluded, the countryside was still a wonderful place, a beautiful setting, where I had often wandered with infinite joy.

Over the years I have found great delight in capturing on film the picturesque landscapes, the old barns, the farms and the remnants of rural life that still survive, reminding us of how things were in days gone by. For no matter how excessive the change may be, the enduring charm of the woods and the fields will always remain a far cry from those concrete streets I knew so well as an urchin child in London.

David Johnston went on to become a Sussex photographer. His photographs make up a collection of over 10,000 colour slides of the countryside. His barn and farm building photographs constitute the largest single, private collection in the south of England.

A review in the West Sussex Gazette in 1999 reads: 'His stunning photographs reveal him to be a worthy successor to the great George Garland, the near-legendary West Sussex photographer who preserved for ever images from the five decades to the 1960s.'

His eminent book West Sussex Barns & Farm Buildings displays the deep care he has for the land he lives in and for the old farm buildings themselves – a heritage that he sees disappearing.